MARRIAGE, THE CHRISTIAN WAY

BUILDING A CHRISTIAN MARRIAGE

RALPH G. BOWLES

Copyright © Ralph G. Bowles 2025.

Crystal Street Press, PO Box 97, Mapleton Queensland 4560, Australia.
crystalstreetpress@icloud.com

ISBN Paperback: 978-1-7638751-0-4 Ebook: 978-1-7638751-1-1

All rights reserved. No part of this book may be reproduced in any form or by any electronic or mechanical means, including information storage and retrieval systems, without written permission from the author, except for the use of brief quotations in a book review. No generative artificial intelligence (AI) was used in the writing of this work. Without in any way limiting the author's exclusive rights under copyright, any use of this publication to 'train' AI technologies to generate text is expressly prohibited. The author reserves all rights to license uses of this work for generative AI training and development of machine learning language models.

Extracts marked BCP are from The Book of Common Prayer, the rights in which are vested in the Crown, and are reproduced by permission of the Crown's patentee, Cambridge University Press. Quotations marked AAPB are from An Australian Prayer Book, Copyright © 1978 by The Anglican Church of Australia Trust Corporation. Used by permission. Quotations marked APBA are from A Prayer Book for Australia, Copyright © 1995 by Broughton Publishing. Used by permission.

Scripture quotations marked **CEB** are from the Common English Bible. Scripture quotations marked **NASB** taken from the (NASB®) New American Standard Bible®, Copyright © 1960, 1971, 1977, 1995, 2020 by The Lockman Foundation. Used by permission. All rights reserved. lockman.org Scripture quotations marked **CEV** are from the Contemporary English Version Copyright © 1991, 1992, 1995 by American Bible Society. Used by Permission. Scripture quotations marked **NIV** are taken from the Holy Bible, New International Version®, NIV®. Copyright © 1973, 1978, 1984, 2011 by Biblica, Inc.™ Used by permission of Zondervan. All rights reserved worldwide. www.zondervan.com The "NIV" and "New International Version" are trademarks registered in the United States Patent and Trademark Office by Biblica, Inc.™ Scripture quotations marked **REB** taken from the Revised English Bible, copyright © Cambridge University Press and Oxford University Press 1989. All rights reserved. Scripture quotations marked **HCSB** are taken from the Holman Christian Standard Bible®, Copyright © 1999, 2000, 2002, 2003 by Holman Bible Publishers. Used by permission. Holman Christian Standard Bible®, Holman CSB®, and HCSB® are federally registered trademarks of Holman Bible Publishers.

Cover images via Bigstock copyright © Licsiren, pellinni

For Sylvia,
with love and appreciation
for your partnership with me
in the 'building' of our marriage,
in the Lord.

CONTENTS

WHAT IS A CHRISTIAN MARRIAGE?	1
The Christian way of marriage	2
The plan of this book: building a Christian marriage	2
Who are these studies for?	3
How to use this book	4
An invitation to build your life, and your marriage, on God's wisdom	7

PART 1
THE DESIGN OF YOUR MARRIAGE

1. A CHRISTIAN MARRIAGE CEREMONY	11
Five parts of the marriage service	12
Reflection/Discussion: A Christian marriage ceremony	17
2. HOLY MATRIMONY IS THE UNION OF A MAN AND A WOMAN	18
The creational bi-unity of humans	19
Sexual union and potential for reproduction	20
Marriage: a union of bodies and lives, for society	21
Reflection/Discussion: Holy matrimony is the union of a man and a woman	22
3. THE THREE PURPOSES OF MARRIAGE	23
Purpose 1. Love-making	23
Purpose 2. Life-making	25
Purpose 3. Life-uniting	28
Reflection/Discussion: The three purposes of marriage	28

4. MARRIAGE IS A PUBLIC LEGAL
   COVENANT   30
   A public commitment   30
   A legal commitment   31
   The Christian life: a public commitment   32
   Reflection/Discussion: Marriage is a public,
   legal covenant   33

5. SEX BELONGS IN MARRIAGE   34
   What sex is for   34
   Living together before marriage?   35
   The biblical ethic of sexual intercourse   36
   The three purposes of sexual union   37
   Sex as expression of Love seeks the good of the
   other   39
   Reflection/Discussion: Sex belongs in marriage   40

6. IN MARRIAGE, A NEW FAMILY IS
   ESTABLISHED   41
   Family life and the one-flesh union   42
   Marriage without children is still marriage   42
   Children, a reminder of your marriage's bigger
   purpose   43
   The 'ghost families' in your marriage   43
   Reflection/Discussion: In marriage, a new
   family is established   44

7. MARRIAGE CONTAINS A MYSTERY   45
   Love is giving ourselves to the other   46
   Deep and close personal union   47
   The Christian good news and our response
   to God   48
   Reflection/Discussion: Marriage contains a
   mystery   49

PART 2
CONSTRUCTING A STRONG MARRIAGE

8. THE PROMISE TO LOVE — 53
- Commitment to love in the future — 54
- Marriage is built by keeping your promises — 55
- Reflection/Discussion: The promise to love — 56

9. TO LOVE, HONOUR, AND PROTECT — 57
- Honouring God — 58
- Never forget the respect due to the beloved — 59
- Reflection/Discussion: To love, honour, and protect — 60

10. FORSAKING ALL OTHERS — 61
- You promise to protect the marriage — 62
- The Christian's exclusive allegiance to the Lord — 63
- Reflection/Discussion: Forsaking all others — 64

11. BE FAITHFUL TO YOUR SPOUSE — 65
- Faithfulness in the Christian life — 66
- Faithfulness—tested by temptations — 67
- Invest in your relationship — 68
- Reflection/Discussion: Be faithful to your spouse — 69

12. A LIFELONG UNION — 70
- Lifetime commitments — 71
- Realism about the future — 71
- Lifelong commitments: marriage and following the Lord — 72
- Marriages have stages — 75
- The spiritual life has its changes and stages — 75
- Reflection/Discussion: A lifelong union — 76

PART 3
ORGANISING YOUR MARRIED LIFE TOGETHER

13. YOUR MARRIAGE IS A SPECIAL KIND OF
    FRIENDSHIP 81
    Becoming good companions 82
    Communication: listening and talking 82
    Constructive conflict resolution 83
    Cooperative attitude 84
    Companionship with God 84
    Cooperating with God 85
    Reflection/Discussion: Your marriage is a
    special kind of friendship 86

14. MARRIAGE ROLES 87
    Marriage structure in biblical days 88
    Headship and submission today? 91
    A proposal for spiritual headship 92
    Reflection/Discussion: Marriage roles 94

15. KEEPING GOD'S COMMANDS IN A
    DIFFERENT ERA 95
    Our contemporary Western marriage context 96
    Marriage: the structure and the spirit 96
    Similar Bible application issues 97
    Reflection/Discussion: Keeping God's
    commands in a different era 98

16. THE WIFE AND HER HUSBAND 100
    A different kind of 'submission' 101
    No place for abuse of the other in marriage 102
    Service is the way of love 104
    Reflection/Discussion: The wife and her
    husband 105

PART 4
DECORATION—FILLING YOUR
MARRIAGE WITH LOVE

17. GROWING TOGETHER IN MARRIAGE	109
Lifelong growth into oneness	110
Knowing Christ and knowing Him better	111
Growing in closeness in your marriage	112
Draw closer to the Lord, draw closer to one another	113
Reflection/Discussion: Growing together in marriage	114
18. THE TWO BECOME ONE—BY ABANDONING SELFISHNESS	115
The two become one flesh	116
Your self does not disappear	116
The 'me' and the 'we' join	117
The Christian parallels: two becoming one	118
Union with Christ	119
The 'we' dimension of love	120
Reflection/Discussion: The two become one—by abandoning selfishness	122
19. THE TWO BECOME ONE—BY JOINING TWO WHOLE PEOPLE	123
Losing your self?	124
Selfhood is not selfishness	125
Giving ourselves, gaining a new self	126
The service—the self-giving—that sets us free	127
Reflection/Discussion: The two become one—by joining two whole people	127
20. THE TWO BECOME ONE—BY UNCONDITIONAL LOVE	129
The commitment line holds steady	130
'For worse'	131
The Christian life has its 'worse'	131

Life can be a battlefield, spiritually	132
Reflection/Discussion: The two become one—by unconditional love	133

21. **MARRIAGE AND THE TWO KINDS OF LOVE** — 134
    - Natural love and supernatural love, gifts from God — 135
    - God's kind of love — 136
    - Reflection/Discussion: Marriage and the two kinds of love — 138

22. **THE TWO BECOME ONE—BY FULFILLING EACH OTHER** — 139
    - Find your fulfilment in the flourishing of your partner — 140
    - Love that fulfils us — 141
    - Reflection/Discussion: The two become one—by fulfilling each other — 142

23. **THE TWO BECOME ONE—BY MUTUAL SUBMISSION OF WILLS** — 143
    - A declaration of non-independence — 144
    - The surprising grace of submission — 144
    - Two wills can work in harmony — 145
    - Reflection/Discussion: The two become one—by mutual submission of wills — 147

PART 5
MAINTENANCE—KEEPING YOUR MARRIAGE IN GOOD REPAIR

24. **RESOLVING CONFLICT IN YOUR MARRIAGE** — 151
    - Learn about each other before you marry — 152
    - Learn to handle conflict constructively — 152
    - Prepare to deal with your conflicts — 154
    - Your 'Constructive Conflict' vow — 154
    - Reflection/Discussion: Resolving conflict in your marriage — 155

25. FORGIVENESS AND YOUR MARRIAGE	156
Forgiving the other may be the hardest marriage task	157
The Christian way of forgiveness	157
Forgiveness and reconciliation	160
The 'Forgiveness Loop'	161
Reflection/Discussion: Forgiveness and your marriage	162
26. WHAT BREAKS A MARRIAGE?	163
Divorce: a contentious issue for the Christian churches	164
Summary	169
Reflection/Discussion: What breaks a marriage?	169
27. REPAIRING YOUR MARRIAGE	171
Daily recommitment	171
The Christian's daily recommitment to God	172
Maintaining your marriage	173
Reflection/Discussion: Repairing your marriage	176

PART 6
REBUILDING YOUR MARRIAGE

28. RESTARTING YOUR MARRIAGE	179
Four steps to rebuilding a marriage	180
Reflection/Discussion: Restarting your marriage	182

PART 7
HOSPITALITY—YOUR MARRIAGE AND ITS GUESTS

29. YOUR MARRIAGE AS A MINISTRY TO OTHERS	187
Four ways a Christian marriage serves the Lord and His world	188
Reflection/Discussion: Your marriage as a ministry to others	192

30. YOUR MARRIAGE AND THE POWER
    OF GOD 193
    Marriages need divine help! 193
    Prayer as the best gift for the couple 194
    Make prayer together part of your married life ... 195
    Watch out for the relationship issues that block
    your prayers 196
    Reflection/Discussion: Your marriage and the
    power of God 197

31. YOUR MARRIAGE AND GOD: THE
    THREE-PLY CORD 198
    Your love for the Lord and your love for one
    another 200
    Two prayers for our marriage 203
    Reflection/Discussion: Your marriage and
    God: the three-ply cord 206

    FINAL THOUGHTS 207

    References and Reading 209
    Thanks 213
    About the Author 215

WHAT IS A CHRISTIAN MARRIAGE?

As society moves further from the Christian worldview, concepts of marriage are changing. The values and practices of the world around us are seeping into the minds of many church people. God's design for marriage is in danger of being forgotten or compromised. Today, fewer people in Western societies marry in a Christian context—or at all.

What does the Christian faith bring to the understanding and practice of marriage?

This book explores the distinctive, biblical, Christian understanding of marriage.

In my work as a Christian pastor for forty-four years, I have been involved in preparing couples for their wedding and for their life together. I have always seen this as a strategically important task and have been ready to give many hours to each couple. Successful marriages are a great source of blessing to society.

I believe the Christian faith and its way of life has much to offer anyone who wants to build a strong and satisfying marriage.

There is a resonance between a marriage that works well—

whatever the religious beliefs of the couple—and the central themes of the Christian religion and way of life.

Like an overture to a symphony or the theme music in a movie, a good marriage plays the theme melodies found in the Christian faith. Find a successful marriage, and you will hear themes of the Christian faith and way of life, playing in a different key.

The melodies of a loving marriage will also attune your ears to the beautiful music of the Christian good news. Understand what a good marriage looks like, and you will see a picture of what is involved in knowing God, as the Christian gospel teaches.

Understand what following Jesus Christ involves, and you will be ready to follow the Maker's instructions for marriage.

The Christian way of marriage

My first aim in this book is to present God's design for marriage as taught in the Bible and as expressed in the marriage services of the Anglican Church (specifically, the Anglican Church of Australia). These marriage services embody the wisdom of long reflection on what it means to be married according to God's way. The other aim of this book is to offer some guidance on how to 'build from the plan' of God as married life develops.

You don't have to be an Anglican to benefit from these studies. Anglican services draw on biblical foundations and a long tradition of Christian understanding. The understanding of marriage outlined in these services shares much in common with Christians from other traditions.

The plan of this book: building a Christian marriage

When a couple gets married, they are *building* a marriage relationship, a life together, and usually a family. It is like building a house, furnishing it, maintaining it, making a home of love in it, and offering hospitality in it.

It is a joint construction by the couple, which starts before their wedding day. How well will they build their marriage, and maintain it over the years?

The Bible book of Proverbs uses a building metaphor to speak about how your life should be constructed and furnished by God's wisdom for life: 'Wisdom has built her house; she has carved out her seven pillars' (Proverbs 9:1-8, CEB).

Applying this metaphor to the building of your marriage, I have organised the material into seven sections.

1. **Design**: the plan of your marriage.
2. **Construction**: the solid materials for building your marriage.
3. **Organisation**: how your married life will operate.
4. **Decoration**: the beauty of married love.
5. **Maintenance**: keeping your marriage in good repair.
6. **Rebuilding**: if your marriage seriously fails.
7. **Hospitality:** how your marriage offers help and hope to others.

As you read and reflect on these studies, I hope you will see how the Christian faith illuminates the nature of marriage and provides resources for building a stronger marriage relationship.

Who are these studies for?

Christian couples preparing for marriage: Engaged couples who are sincere, active followers of Jesus Christ will have a particular concern to express their faith in their married life together. Read this book together and discuss the material.

Couples who are getting married in a Christian church service: These studies will help you gain a deeper understanding of your wedding service and how the Christian faith can help your marriage. You don't have to be a church member or follower of Jesus Christ to benefit. Since God designed marriage for humanity generally, the Bible's teaching will be relevant to those who do not have allegiance to Christian beliefs.

Married couples: Newlywed couples may use these studies for shared discussion as they start out on their married life-journey. The material can also be used by married couples who want to refresh their insights into God's design for marriage, or prepare for public or private renewal of their marriage vows.

Pastors: Marriage celebrants who are planning a wedding service and preparing a couple for their marriage can use this book to help the couple understand the nature of the Christian faith and its application to marriage.

Christian small groups: Your study group can use these studies for a series on the biblical vision of marriage.

How to use this book

Each study explores one facet of marriage. They may be completed as a month of daily studies, or on any schedule that suits you.

Each study ends with questions for individual reflection or for discussion together.

The book moves from the foundational design of marriage in the Christian Way through the development of marriage, to the challenges that marriages face, and the ministry of marriage in the Lord. You can, of course, start in any section.

Books for further reading are listed at the end of the studies. References in the text refer to books on this list.

I hope that all readers will see how an understanding of

marriage illuminates what it means to be in relationship with God through Jesus Christ, and how a relationship with God can help you get more out of your marriage.

Ralph G. Bowles
2025

AN INVITATION TO BUILD YOUR LIFE, AND YOUR MARRIAGE, ON GOD'S WISDOM

Wisdom has built her house with its seven columns. She has prepared the meat and set out the wine.

Her feast is ready.

She has sent her servant women to announce her invitation from the highest hills:

'Everyone who is ignorant or foolish is invited! All of you are welcome to my meat and wine. If you want to live, give up your foolishness and let understanding guide your steps.'

PROVERBS 9:1-6 (CEV)

PART 1
THE DESIGN OF YOUR MARRIAGE

Every house is built according to a plan, and the Christian idea of marriage follows a design found in the Bible and expressed in church wedding services.

1 A CHRISTIAN MARRIAGE CEREMONY

A Christian wedding ceremony shows the shape of a Christian marriage.

Engaged couples want a picturesque, attractive setting for their wedding ceremony. Churches have often been selected because the building is grand and impressive, with stone walls, vaulted ceilings, stained glass, and organ music.

I was the minister in a parish where one of the church buildings was a humble hall, rather like a cross between a Scout Hall and an electricity sub-station. I took a phone call enquiry about a wedding booking for that building, and I asked the woman first up: 'You haven't seen our church building, have you?' When she checked it out, the booking didn't proceed.

These days more couples are getting married in civil ceremonies with no connection to church, so the chosen setting may be a garden, or a mountain-top with a majestic view.

It is not the building or the place, the flowers or the music, however, that make a *Christian* wedding ceremony. It is the *meaning* of the service itself. Nowadays, the Christian religion, the meaning of a Christian wedding service, and the distinctive Christian view of marriage are less familiar to many.

In this first section, we will study the ground-plan or design of the 'house' of marriage. The architectural plan is not the house, but it will decide the shape and function of the home you are building. It is important to have a good foundational design and God, the Designer of marriage, has provided one.

Five parts of the marriage service

Let's have a look at the Christian wedding service, as found in the Anglican church tradition. You will notice that there are at least five parts to the marriage service. (There are some variations in the order of these components in the different versions of the marriage service, but they are all there.)

1. The worship of God

The couple's marriage is held in a setting of Christian worship. It is not only the wedding couple who is the focus, but the Lord God, too. This may be missed by many in the excitement of the ceremony, where the focus is on the happy couple.

At one wedding I conducted many years ago, the couple astonished me by talking softly to each other throughout much of the service, as if the words of the service, my address, the hymns, and the prayers, were mere backdrop to their own interaction. I was addressing my remarks to them, as well as the assembled congregation, but they were not paying attention. It was disconcerting, to say the least.

For those who take God seriously, however, this context of worship is very significant. The opening words of the service are a greeting in the Lord's name or an exhortation, such as: 'We have come together here in the sight of God and in the presence of this congregation...' (Marriage AAPB First Form, 548).

Psalms, Christian hymns and songs, and prayers also surround the couple's commitment to one another.

The marrying couple comes before God to make these promises; God, as well as the people who are present, is a witness to the wedding. This reminds us immediately that marriage is a part of life that is under God's direction, and we can look for help in married life from God, the Designer of marriage.

2. Listening to the Word of God

The focus of the Christian service is not just on the love of the couple for each other. Their love is set in a larger frame of Love—the love of God for us in Christ.

The biblical purposes of marriage are proclaimed at the beginning of the service. Readings from the Bible and a sermon on marriage set the vows in the perspective of God and His purposes.

The 'Ministry of the Word' comes after the vows in some marriage services, but it also fits well preceding the vows, as in *A Prayer Book for Australia*. After the meaning of the vows is explained, the couple proceeds to make them.

The calling of the couple to love and cherish each other is seen to express the deeper meaning of the 'one flesh' union of man and woman which we will look at in Study 2, and provides the foundation of family life within the covenant of marriage.

3. The wedding vows

The heart of the marriage service is the covenant commitment of the groom and the bride to each other. They do not say 'I love you'; they say: 'I *will* love you'. They are not only *declaring* their love; they are also *promising* to love each other from this day on.

The vows are strong and involve complete commitment. The nature of their love-commitment and how it will shape their future together is expressed in the vows.

I have been asked, sometimes, to allow the couple to replace the vows in the Anglican service with their own set of words. I have declined this request because the couple have come for a *Christian* ceremony, and these vows carry the Christian view of marriage. They express the covenant (promise) essence of marriage.

If the couple want to include other personal promises to each other, this can be included at other places in the ceremony or the celebrations.

4. The declaration of the marriage

Marriage is not a private matter but a public commitment, with social and legal recognition.

The minister declares the couple to be husband and wife when they have exchanged their vows. A covenant union has been enacted by these vows, and covenants usually have witnesses. The marriage covenant has been made before God as witness, and before others.

A covenant is a solemn commitment between people. This is not a light commitment they are making. Their commitment is witnessed legally by attending witnesses and the official celebrant representing the State. Their union of marriage is registered legally with the government by signing the certificates during or immediately after the service.

A wedding ceremony is a public occasion. Marriage is more than a private arrangement between the couple. Most of us know friends who have moved in together and we usually hear about it later; we don't hear them explain the nature of their commitment to each other beforehand, or in front of a group. They tell us (or we hear) that they have moved in together, but the nature of their commitment to each other is not explained.

In a marriage service and ceremony, however, the couple make their commitment publicly, in front of others, and sign their names to it.

The groom and the bride make their 'solemn vow and promise', 'in the presence of God'. The giving of the rings, with the promise to honour each other 'with all that I am and all that I have', is done 'in the name of God' (Marriage APBA First Order, 649).

In former times people usually took vows before God very seriously. To take a vow—make a promise—before God, is to ask God to watch your performance of your promise and hold you accountable (see Ecclesiastes 5:1-2).

You are making a commitment not just to one another, but to God Himself.

5. The prayers

The Christian marriage service includes blessings and prayers for the couple. The people of God, including, usually, the families and friends of the couple, pray to God to bless them and guide them in their married life.

Filled with their fresh love for each other, the newlyweds tend to be idealistic about the future of their marriage. Their love will carry them through!

Prayer surrounding their wedding should be a reminder that they will need help to keep their promises, and that God, the Designer of marriage, can be a real practical help.

The prayers in the wedding service may seem like nice background, but the time may come when prayer becomes a lifeline for a sinking relationship. I know from my pastoral experience that married partners can reach a point of desperate prayer that God would help them in their marriage.

Christian couples will know that their praying friends will continue to uphold them before God after the ceremony. Why not specifically ask some of your close, trusted friends to intercede for your marriage as prayer-partners? This may bring blessings that surprise you and help that supports you.

Distinctive differences of a Christian wedding service:

- It has a Godward focus.
- It is enclosed in a worship service: it is an act of worship.
- It is framed by the Bible's teaching.
- It is a solemn act of commitment (covenant) witnessed by God and others.
- It is surrounded by prayers.

These distinctives of a Christian marriage service may be just background for many wedding couples, like the pretty flowers, gorgeous dresses, and beautiful stained glass. For those who follow Christ, they are at the heart of their mutual marriage commitment.

A Christian wedding ceremony lays out the ground-plan for the marriage you are building in the Lord. The service contains the design of a Christian marriage for the days, weeks, months, years, and, hopefully, decades to follow.

What happens in the wedding service should happen in the everyday life of the couple who want to build a Christian marriage: placing the worship of God at the centre of your relationship and family.

- Look to the Bible, the Word of God, to be your wisdom for life.
- Trust God as a couple and family for the day-to-day challenges of life.
- Make prayer part of your relationship and family life.

- Keep your relationship connected to the fellowship of God's people.

In coming chapters, we will draw out more wisdom from the Christian tradition for the blessings and challenges of married life.

Reflection/Discussion: A Christian marriage ceremony

1. Read one of the marriage services in an Anglican prayer book. What strikes you as you read it? What is not clear to you?
2. You have chosen to exchange your marriage vows in a Christian ceremony and context. What are the differences between a civil ceremony and a church wedding?

2 HOLY MATRIMONY IS THE UNION OF A MAN AND A WOMAN

In designing marriage, God the Creator has put together some vital elements for human flourishing that we should not separate.

When I started conducting wedding services in 1981, I never dreamed that this opening statement would one day become controversial for many people:

> 'We have come together in the sight of God for the joining in marriage of this man N and this woman N.'
> (Marriage AAPB Second Form, 560)

The biblical definition of marriage as the union of two distinct 'forms' of human persons (male and female) is under challenge these days.

Even the definition of what is a man and what is a woman has become controversial. I didn't see that coming when I started doing weddings!

In these studies, I am staying with the traditional Christian and biblical view of marriage: the life-union of a man (an adult human biological male) and a woman (an adult human biological female).

The creational bi-unity of humans

The Bible defines marriage as the union of a man and a woman. This is found in all strata of the Bible, from the first book (Genesis) to the New Testament. It was the teaching of Jesus Christ:

> 'Our Lord Jesus Christ said of marriage that "From the beginning of creation God made them male and female. 'For this reason, a man shall leave his father and mother and be joined to his wife, and the two shall become one.'"' (Marriage AAPB Second Form, 560)

Why does the Bible describe marriage as the union of a man and a woman?

The reason is straightforward. It is only in the sexual and personal union of a man and a woman that a child can be produced, and (usually) nurtured. It is the sexual union that produces children. Marriage is designed to be a *procreative* union.

Humans come in two kinds, male and female, defined by capacity for reproduction. 'Mankind exists in the female-male duality as a creational given' (Olthuis, 4). The biblical understanding of male and female is defined by the complementary task of reproduction.

This is the foundational meaning of how the two become 'one flesh': the two humans do something as one unit physically ('flesh').

Humankind is a bi-unity. The union of marriage in the Bible is not the uniting of two same kinds of beings (man and man, woman and woman). Marriage is to be a union of two *biologically complementary* human beings because reproduction and the nurture of offspring is one of the main purposes of marriage.

Sexual union and potential for reproduction

There is a trend in Western societies at present to define maleness and femaleness in terms of feelings or self-identification. The biblical definition, however, is grounded in the reproductive sexual complementarity, which is the foundation of society since it is from sexual union that children come. Male and female in the biblical view of marriage are not defined by their feelings but by their creaturely, biological reality, with the capacity for sexual union and potential for reproduction.

The foundational text in the Bible that describes the creation of humans as male and female provides the explanation for their maleness and femaleness as their joint task: 'God blessed them and said to them, "Be fertile and multiply; fill the earth and master it"' (Genesis 1:28, CEB).

The complementary union of the man and the woman is seen in the sexual realm by the physical 'fit' of their reproductive and sexual systems. The reproductive act is a joint physical act that requires both a man and a woman to do it. This obvious, undeniable fact of nature/creation is basic to the Christian understanding of marriage.

It is also an emotional or *personal* union between the man and the woman, who are attracted to each other, although they are different in some ways. Their sexual union is not only *procreative* (or potentially so); the union of their bodies expresses their personal union of lives.

In marriage we are not seeking union with a being that is a replica of ourselves, but one who is both like us, yet 'other'. 'Love presupposes that the other is truly other, is not simply an extension of my being, and thus never "mine" … In love the other becomes truly "Thou", enabling me to become "I"'

(Hall, 156). The complementary union is also expressed in the emotional and relational dimensions as the two different sexes balance and support each other.

The mating of the man and the woman provides the natural and best environment for the nurture of any children born to the couple. Children do not just need parents to cause their existence; they need parents to protect, nurture, and guide them.

As parents, the two sexes also provide models of a man/father, and a woman/mother for their offspring, through the process of identification.

Marriage: a union of bodies and lives, for society

Right at the beginning of the Bible's teaching about marriage as the union of a man and a woman, then, we find three strands woven together:

- The sexual union draws the two significantly different kinds of humans towards each other to do something creative together that each can't do on their own: to bring new human beings into the world.
- The fruit or result of their sexual and life union is usually the production of children.
- The joining of their lives together in love and mutual support (the two become one unit) makes the bond that provides the foundation for secure family life.

This is why marriage has been designed as the union of man and woman according to the Bible. It brings together and keeps together, in the bond of marriage, the sexual act, the personal life-union, and the production and care of children.

We all know that these *can* be separated. The biblical call is that they *ought not* to be separated.

Sexual intercourse, of course, can happen outside of a life-union, and without love. Emotional and personal love can happen without the procreative act of sexual union. Children can be raised outside of the marriage union, conceived outside of a life-union of man and woman, and even conceived without the act of sexual intercourse—although the created potential for a human life (the egg of the female and the sperm of the male) must be there.

Society now often separates sex from life-union or love; and love-unions are separated from the created reproductive union. Conception is sometimes separated from the sexual act itself. There is a direct clash between current trends about sex, gender, marriage, reproduction, and family, and the biblical and Christian way of marriage.

Marriage in the biblical view keeps together the three components: sexual union, life-union, and family-foundation. Jesus said that what God has joined together, people must not separate: humans must not pull apart what God has put together (Matthew 19:6).

Pulling apart what God/nature puts together often leads to poor outcomes.

We will take a closer look at the interconnected purposes for marriage in the next chapter.

Reflection/Discussion: Holy matrimony is the union of a man and a woman

1. Why do you think the Christian, biblical teaching holds that marriage is between a man and a woman?
2. What is missing in a same-sex union compared to biblical and traditional marriage?

3 THE THREE PURPOSES OF MARRIAGE

Marriage in God's design has a general threefold purpose, for our blessing.

Our society in the West has seen significant redefining of marriage in recent decades, and even the idea of 'man' and 'woman' is contested. In the biblical view, however, marriage is designed by God and should not be reinvented or redesigned by people.

The marriage service begins with a statement of the purposes of marriage as taught in the Bible. It is a special relationship that has been ordained by God. There are three main purposes listed in the Anglican marriage services for which marriage was 'instituted by God' (Marriage AAPB Second Form, 560).

Marriage, by God's design, is for *love-making*, *life-creating*, and *life-uniting*.

Purpose 1. Love-making

People use the phrase 'making love' to refer to a couple having sexual intercourse, but we all know that the sex act can happen without love. In the biblical view, sex and love should go together, and the Christian view of marriage places sexual intercourse in the protective shelter of committed love.

Marriage is the place for the proper expression of sexual desires—the 'natural instincts and affections with which He has endowed us' (Marriage AAPB Second Form, 560).

The marriage covenant and the sexual union belong together. When the man and the woman become *one flesh* in the Genesis account of marriage (Genesis 2:24), one important aspect of this joining of their lives was their sexual union.

We know that there can be 'casual sex' and understand that it does not mean there is love or life-commitment. Sexual intercourse when it operates outside the covenant union of marriage may only create a union of bodies, not the one-flesh union of marriage. This is the helpful distinction made by the apostle Paul in one of his letters in the New Testament (1 Corinthians 6:16-20).

The plan of God is for the act of sexual union to take place within the commitment of two lives to one another. The union of the two bodies sexually is to be part of the union of the two lives.

Sexual intercourse is designed by God to express on a physical level the joining of the two lives. 'Sexual union is the physical climax of personal union between a man and a woman' (Atkinson, 1979, 28).

In the biblical and Christian view then, the sexual act is more than a physical action. It has a *sacramental* significance; the physical union should express a union of hearts and lives.

Christians know that physical actions can become 'sacraments' through which we experience spiritual meaning and blessing. A sacrament is more than a sign; it brings with it some experience of the sign's reality. In the Holy Communion, the act of consuming bread and wine conveys our participation in the saving work of Jesus Christ in his death for sins.

The married couple's loving joining of their bodies sexually seals and expresses their love-and-life union. Their sexual union in a loving, committed relationship functions in a sacramental way for the couple, expressing in the joining of their bodies the joining of their lives in love, and being a physical experience of this loving union.

So, it is important to keep marriage and sex together, and in the right order. Notice the sequence in Genesis 2: the uniting of the lives of the man and the woman comes first, and then they join sexually into one flesh. This is why Christians want to keep sexual union inside the marriage union.

Here is a big contrast between the Christian view of sex and marriage, and the current social consensus in secular Western society. The Christian views sex as reserved for the marriage covenant—not for recreation, dating, passing romances, or even for serious relationships without the life-commitment of marriage.

The Christian's approach to sexual intercourse does not mean it is devalued. The opposite is the case; we place it in a high and precious place of significance, reserving it for loving life-commitment.

Should a couple live together before they make a marriage commitment? The Christian ethic of sex and marriage rules this out, placing life-commitment before sexual union, and total commitment before partial or reserved commitment.

Despite the widespread belief that living together before marriage increases the chances of a lasting and happy marriage, the statistical evidence points to the opposite. Cohabitation before marriage leads to less stable marriages.

The biblical plan for marriage works best in practice.

Love-making is for marriage.

Purpose 2. Life-making

Marriage is designed to be the place where family life happens, 'so that children may be born and nurtured in secure and loving care, for their well-being and instruction, and for the good order of society, to the glory of God' (Marriage AAPB Second Form, 561).

The couple are called 'one flesh' because in their sexual union they act jointly to do something each cannot do on their own—create a human being.

Marriage is for *life-making*—new lives begotten as the offspring of the union. The words of the service here are definite: God wants children to be cared for and raised in the best environment. God's plan is that children be raised and nurtured in the secure relationship of a committed, covenant relationship between the two parents.

Bearing and raising children is a responsibility from God. Children are not objects for our self-fulfilment; they are *our responsibility* for *their* fulfilment.

In having children, the love of the married couple creates a new love out of their love, a new little person who represents their union, even their very physical selves in noticeable ways. Leon Kass puts this memorably: 'Flesh of their flesh, the child is the parents' own commingled being externalized and given a separate and persisting existence' (Kass, 12). In a real, physical and personal way, the child is the fruit of their loving union.

The parents then want to give a good life to the life they have procreated.

Many people think that having children can be taken right out of the marriage union; some even deliberately thwart the natural pattern of family life (a father and a mother).

When we separate what God puts together (marriage and parenting), the results usually mean unhappiness and insecurity. Children raised in situations outside of a stable marriage relationship with both their biological parents are more likely to be exposed to abuse. According to research assembled by the Witherspoon Institute based in Princeton, New Jersey, the more that marriage is weakened as the context for sexual union and the raising of children, the more exposed children will be to possible harm.

Sex outside marriage often means children outside marriage. Children in loosely bonded cohabiting or casual-relationship families are exposed to worse outcomes. In Newark, New Jersey, USA, 605 of the children in the city were found to be growing up in families without fathers. Higher violence and social problems followed. 'One study found that boys reared in single-parent and stepfamilies were more than twice as likely to end up in prison, compared to boys reared in an intact family' (*Marriage and the Public Good: Ten Principles, III. The Well-Being of Children*).

While marriage as a committed life-union is the God-designed context for the birth and raising of children, this does not always happen. A true marriage as a covenant life-union can exist without the arrival of children, as is the reality in every marriage before any child is born.

There are marriages where the couple are childless for years, and sometimes the couple never see the arrival of children. There may also be good reasons why a couple should not seek to have children.

Marriage can have a general purpose of producing children, as God's design for humanity, but for some marriages this does not happen. The Bible itself has examples of marriages in which the couple cannot conceive children, and there is no doubt about the validity of such marriages.

A married couple who are unable to conceive their own children can provide the foundational union for the adoption or fostering of children who do not have a secure parental home.

Marriage is the best place for *creating lives*.

Purpose 3. Life-uniting

Marriage is designed to be 'a lifelong union in which a man and a woman are called so to give themselves in body, mind and spirit, and so to respond, that from their union will grow a deepening knowledge and love for each other' (Marriage AAPB Second Form, 560).

Marriage is for life-building—the building up of the life of each partner and the creation of a shared life, *one flesh*. Marriage is to be a total, growing union of loving mutual care and commitment.

'The marriage relationship is intended to be—and increasingly to become—the one-flesh union of total love-commitment, person to person, at all levels of life and experience, symbolized by, expressed in and deepened through sexual union' (Atkinson, 89).

Marriage is a calling to build a union of lives in love.

These three biblical purposes of marriage (love-making, life-making, life-uniting) are God's design for the optimal fulfilment and the well-being of partners, children, families, and society. God wants our best and knows better than us what this optimum requires.

In the third section we will explore the beautiful facets of this one-flesh, growing union of lives.

The next chapter will explain how the *public commitment* of the marriage comes before the *private sexual sealing* of the union.

Reflection/Discussion: The three purposes of marriage

1. Contemporary society has accepted that sexual union can take place outside of, and before, the exchange of marriage commitments. What are the

consequences of this reversal and violation of God's order for marriage?
2. What are *your* purposes for getting married? What do you want from marriage?

4 MARRIAGE IS A PUBLIC LEGAL COVENANT

> Marriage is not just for the couple; it is a public commitment, serving the good of society and affecting the well-being of others.

Why get married? What does a piece of paper do for your relationship? What is the need for a ceremony? Isn't 'living together' really the same thing as marriage? Many couples now live together without a ceremony (Christian or otherwise), and without any legal registration of their relationship.

For the Christian faith, however, 'marriage' is different from 'moving in together'.

A public commitment

Marriage in the Bible, and in most societies down the ages, has been a public commitment, recognised by the community and legally endorsed. From the first biblical reference to marriage, and throughout the whole Bible, it is always a union made publicly in front of witnesses, including God, and marking a leaving of the old family ties for the new bond.

'This is the reason that a man leaves his father and mother and embraces his wife, and they become one flesh.' (Genesis 2:24, CEB)

In biblical marriages, the oaths and public commitments are made before the sexual union and joining together (see Ruth 3; 4:9-13; Genesis 24; 29:28-30; Ezekiel 16:8,59; Deuteronomy 20:7; Luke 1:26-27).

The biblical word for this kind of relationship is *'covenant'*. Marriage is a covenant of commitment between a man and a woman (Malachi 2:14).

In a biblical covenant, there are always witnesses involved. It is the same today with serious contracts and commitments in modern society. Our signatures are witnessed by others to give legal force to the covenant.

God is also a witness to biblical marriages (Genesis 2:24; Malachi 2:14). This is why the Church has celebrated marriages in the context of prayer and public vows in the presence of witnesses; 'before God and this company', as the old wedding service says.

A private relationship that is undertaken without any witnesses or recognition by society or law is not a marriage *covenant*.

A legal commitment

Marriage in biblical thought is a binding legal union (Romans 7:2). The legal basis of marriage in the Bible (and in most societies) can be seen in the reality of divorce. When a marriage is over, there must be a legal endorsement of this ending (Deuteronomy 24:1-4).

Marriage is not just for the couple; it is for the good of society and affects the well-being of others. This is why marriage is a legal commitment with obligations and protection under law.

The Christian marriage service includes the signing of official documents before witnesses and before an authorised agent of the government. The State and the community have an interest in marriage as a social institution because it is integral to the welfare of our society and people.

The Christian life: a public commitment

The public and solemn commitment of marriage can also be seen when you compare it with the Christian's commitment to God. The Christian disciple enters a union with Christ that is total, unreserved, binding, and public.

When a person is baptised as a follower of Christ, it is a public event, involving promises/vows, with witnesses. It is recorded officially by the church and a certificate is issued.

As an Anglican priest, I have officiated at many weddings and conducted many baptisms. I often think of the similarity in these two covenant ceremonies.

At a wedding, as in a baptism, there are two parties making big and solemn promises to each other, for life and love, in front of witnesses, before God.

In a baptism, the Lord makes promises to the disciple in the gospel, and the new disciple makes promises to God.

In a wedding service, the couple make big promises to one another.

The baptism vows resemble the wedding vows. They are both lifelong, all-encompassing, and unconditional promises.

Like Christian baptism, marriage is a covenant commitment. It is not a private arrangement. It is a public event, with legal recognition and public vows, witnessed by others, and, for Christians especially, undertaken before God.

By seeking legal, public, community, and Divine recognition of your marriage relationship, you are binding yourselves to keep your commitments and putting up a clear set of boundaries around your marriage relationship.

After the public commitment is made, the couple will seal their union privately and physically in the act of sexual love.

The next chapter will take a deeper look at how Christ-followers understand the meaning of sexual intercourse in marriage.

Reflection/Discussion: Marriage is a public, legal covenant

1. Can you be married in God's sight without a public ceremony of commitment?
2. Think about how your marriage commitment resembles the commitment of a person to follow Jesus Christ—to become a Christian—a seen, for example, in the act of Christian baptism.

5 SEX BELONGS IN MARRIAGE

The Christian view of sexual intercourse gives it high importance as a God-given blessing and wants to protect it from misuse and devaluation.

One of the biggest points of difference between Christ-followers and contemporary Western morality is their views of sex.

The Western sexual revolution has disconnected sexual union from life-union for many in our society. Sexual intercourse is now regarded as not restricted to marriage. (However, it is worth noting that most people still hold to the importance of sexual fidelity in marriage and committed relationships.)

Even with sexual intercourse, for the best results, follow the Maker's instructions.

What sex is for

The marriage service challenges contemporary values and practices when it affirms the biblical teaching that marriage is God's place for sexual intercourse.

The oldest Anglican marriage service lists sexual intercourse as the first purpose or reason for marriage. It is for the procreation of children, and to be a godly means for the expression of sexual desires (Matrimony BCP, 291). This idea has continued in later versions:

> 'Marriage is a gift from God for the well-being of mankind and for the proper expression of natural instincts and affections with which He has endowed us.' (Marriage AAPB Second Form, 560)

Many years ago, I thought this was a rather low aspect to be the first-cited, basic reason for marriage. Surely, I thought, it is the love-relationship that should be mentioned first, not the sexual union of the couple. The later Anglican marriage services seem to have agreed with my feeling, because they re-ordered the purposes of marriage.

I now see things differently. The listing of the purposes in the older service is correct because the sexual union of the couple is the bodily foundation of the whole relationship and the means of its usual outcome, the production of children—the basic purpose for which our sexual natures are designed.

Living together before marriage?

Should a couple live together before they make a marriage commitment? This is now very common. Sexual union and living together has become the major pathway to marriage in Western societies.

Those who keep their sexual union to their marriage commitment are now mostly found in minority religious groups in Australian society. I have learned that when people find out that Christian engaged couples have not been living together or in a sexual relationship, they are amazed and find it strange, even a bit weird.

Many think that it is a good thing to live together before marriage. However, despite the widespread belief that living together before marriage increases the chances of a lasting and happy marriage, the evidence points to the opposite. Cohabitation before marriage often leads to less stable marriages.

> 'Adults in cohabiting unions face higher rates of domestic violence, sexual infidelity, and instability, compared to couples in marital unions ... Cohabiting unions are typically weaker than marriages and appear more likely to lead to poor relationship outcomes ... Cohabiting unions are particularly risky for children.' (*Marriage and the Public Good: Ten Principles, III.* 'Four Threats to Marriage', 'Cohabitation')

While the biblical plan for marriage may look strange to modern Western eyes, it has real practical benefits. It is good for marital stability and longevity.

The Christian way of sex and marriage is also good for the security of children and the establishment of stable families, the basis of society. The biblical sexual ethic puts sexual union in the context where children born to the couple are likely to be best cared for in a family where a strong and legally recognised relationship has been formed.

The biblical ethic of sexual intercourse

There is a sound and powerful logic to the biblical ethic of sex. Sexual intercourse is good and designed by God, according to the Bible and our Church's teaching. Husband and wife have a sexual duty to each other, to serve the other for their satisfaction in a mutual act of loving sex (1 Corinthians 7:3-5).

It is a false spirituality to think that being sexual excludes being spiritual. There is nothing unclean or shameful about sexual intercourse in itself; it is human distortion of sexuality that is condemned in Scripture.

As a pastor-teacher, I have been concerned for many years that so many churches do not give clear biblical guidelines about sex to the youth in their congregations. I have asked my fellow ministers what systematic teaching they give in their parish program about the ethics of sex, only to find that it has been neglected almost completely. All the while, our society constantly 'preaches' its sexual message to youth and others, on multiple channels.

The three purposes of sexual union

When we understand the biblical purposes for sexual intercourse, we can understand why sexual union belongs in the marriage covenant.

There is a good summary of the Christian ethic of sex in the Anglican church's traditional wedding services. The biblical and traditional view of marriage anchors the Christian sexual ethic.

The marriage service sets out the three purposes for sexual union between a man and a woman, as presented in the Bible:

1. **Life-creating:** sexual intercourse is *a life-creating act*, usually and potentially

Sexual intercourse is the one biological act that the man and the woman do together that they cannot do separately. The two become 'one flesh'—one unit—to create another person.

It is a *generative* union (potentially). It points beyond our own pleasure to the calling to nurture another life. From this union of lives and bodies comes a new family.

Even with widespread use of contraception, sexual intercourse outside marriage often results in babies being born outside a secure and balanced family situation. Unwanted pregnancies then often result, tragically, in the killing of the unborn child.

2. **Life-uniting:** sexual intercourse is *a life-uniting act*

Sexual union is a powerful physical and emotional act of intimacy. It strengthens our emotional connection with each other.

Like a precious gem meant to be set in a gold ring, the sexual act (the uniting of their bodies) should be kept in the context of loving commitment of selves (the uniting of their lives).

Because of its power to connect people, sex can become a substitute for the commitment of the whole person. Sexual intimacy too early in the relationship can subvert the development of a sound personal union. The partners (often the woman) may mistake sexual intimacy for proof of love, which may not be correct. (For further reading see Talley & Reed, 1982.)

The couple join their lives together and seal their union in the joining of their bodies sexually. This is the *sacramental* meaning of the sexual act; it is the physical union expressing the union of lives.

This is the order for the Christ-follower: the *reality* of the union of lives, followed by the *sealing* of the union, the joining of their bodies in sexual union. The act of sexual union sacramentally expresses their love and their uniting.

3. **Love-building:** sexual intercourse is *a love-building act*

Sexual union is more than simply procreative; it builds and expresses love. Sexual intercourse as an expression of love-union gives it meaning beyond the child-bearing years of a marriage, and in cases where conception does not happen.

We all know that sex can happen without love, but when love exists and is expressed in sexual giving, the love-bond is strengthened. For this to happen, the sex must serve the love.

It is not surprising, therefore, that research has found that couples with a secure love-bond in marriage report higher sexual satisfaction than those who have sex in less committed relationships (see Crawford and Butler). When I have pointed out to people how research indicates that love and commitment is the most satisfying setting for sexual fulfilment, they don't want to believe me. Yet this is what repeated surveys have found.

A secure, committed relational bond in marriage provides a good way of keeping together the three purposes of sexual intercourse: love-building; life-uniting; life-creating.

The Bible calls us to honour marriage by avoiding sexual intercourse outside the bond of marriage—either adultery or sex without marriage: marriage must be honoured in every respect, with no cheating on the relationship, because God will judge the sexually immoral person and the person who commits adultery (Hebrews 13:4; see 1 Thessalonians 4:3-5).

Sex as expression of Love seeks the good of the other

The Christian sees sex as an expression of love in the commitment of one's life to the other. This sexual ethic puts a brake on using sex and the sexual partner for one's own pleasure without commitment to them.

This is in tune with the Christian approach to life generally, where we commit ourselves to the well-being of others, and do not use them for our own pleasure. Love 'does not seek its own', says the apostle Paul (1 Corinthians 13:5, NASB).

The Christian way of marriage is strong on commitment as the undergirding of love. It places life-commitment before sexual union, expressing total life-commitment, not partial or reserved, in a bodily way.

It is not surprising that the Bible likens our commitment to God to a marriage: the two parties in full commitment of love to each other, the two becoming one (Ephesians 5:31-32). We will explore this more in later chapters.

If you have not kept your sexual life pure, remember that there is forgiveness and cleansing available through Jesus Christ (Psalm 32:1-5).

Reflection/Discussion: Sex belongs in marriage

1. Think about the three purposes of sexual intercourse according to the Bible. Do you agree that sex is best kept in marriage?
2. How will you keep your sexual life satisfying?

6 IN MARRIAGE, A NEW FAMILY IS ESTABLISHED

Whether your marriage receives the gift of children or not, you are called to build a home that will be the best and natural place for children to flourish.

Years ago, when our children were younger and at home, my wife and I were having a cuppa after work in the lounge room, and she asked me to help her with the script for a drama sketch she was learning for a church service. The script called for a married couple to have an argument; I read the husband's part, and my wife played the wife's part.

We were getting into the roles, with raised voices and strong (acted) emotions. Then, I saw my daughter's face peer slowly around the doorway. She had heard her parents loudly arguing, which was in fact not our custom. The look of concern on her face was unmistakable. We quickly explained that it was only a play, a script.

Parents who are unhappy with each other, whose love is failing, are a worry to their children, whose security depends on their parents' relationship.

The marriage service restates the Bible's teaching that God wants 'children to be born and nurtured in secure and loving care for their well-being and instruction and for the good order of society, to the glory of God' (Marriage AAPB Second Form, 561). A marriage covenant between the parents is God's way of providing the stability and loving environment for the nurture of children.

Family life and the one-flesh union

The world may think that parenting can be detached deliberately from marriages, and that even the male-female complementary roles in parenting can be thwarted. The Christian way of marriage and family life contrasts to this view, strongly connecting the development of the children with the modelling, love, and security of the one-flesh union.

Get yourselves married before you get yourselves children —this is God's way.

The Christian design for marriage regards the establishment of a committed, loving marriage union as the foundation for raising children. This means the primary task for the husband and the wife is to build a strong and healthy marriage upon which to build a family.

Marriage without children is still marriage

The general purpose of marriage in God's design ties the birth and raising of children to the marriage union. To sever this connection may lead to children who lack security and good identification with their parents.

Not every marriage, of course, results in children. The parents may be unable to have children or decide for good reasons that it would be best not to become parents.

Whether you have children or not, you should develop a home that would be good for children if they were part of it, where your love for one another could be seen by them, where kindness and faithfulness fill the home. This is the test of family life.

Children, a reminder of your marriage's bigger purpose

The coming of children into a marriage reminds us that marriage is not just about ourselves. Your marriage is not just for you and your own fulfilment. Marriage is a social institution that is vital for the nurture of children and for the well-being of society.

The well-being of your family life will depend upon the soundness of your marriage. The couple should not make the mistake of allowing the task of parenting to displace the task of keeping their marriage healthy and growing. The well-being of the children will depend greatly on the loving oneness of the parents.

The 'ghost families' in your marriage

The partners in the marriage will bring their own experiences of what a family should or shouldn't be like. These scripts from their families of origin will influence the way the couple proceed to develop their new family. It is helpful to work through the lessons and impact of our family backgrounds as we prepare for marriage and family life.

When my wife and I got married and started our family, we discussed how we would raise our children. We came from families with different approaches to child-rearing, so we needed to work out how we would do this as new parents.

A key aspect for us was how to help our children learn about God. The task of parenting as models and instillers of faith kept us occupied for the growing years of our offspring. Parents cannot avoid the spiritual dimension of nurture. To leave it out is to teach a lesson that this part of life is not important.

How will you live out your beliefs, and what will you model for your children? The issue is unavoidable. For Christ-followers, it is a top priority.

The family that is created from your marriage will be the primary place where your children learn about God. The saying is true: 'God has no grandchildren.' Each child needs to come to his or her own personal connection by faith to God. Parents have an unavoidable role in this question. May the spiritual influence of our parenting reflect the truth and love of God in Christ.

The marriage service includes a prayer for the children that may come from this union:

> 'Grant ... that they and their children may come to know you in their lives and give you praise and honour, through Jesus Christ our Lord.' (Marriage APBA Second Form, 566)

Parents who build a loving marriage in which their children can flourish paint a picture of another relationship: the relationship between God and people.

Reflection/Discussion: In marriage, a new family is established

1. Each partner brings an experience of family life from their family of origin. Have you been able to talk through this background of the new family you are establishing? Have you discussed the issue of children?
2. How will you help your children learn about the Christian faith?

7 MARRIAGE CONTAINS A MYSTERY

There is a secret hidden inside marriage: it is a picture of the relationship of Christ and the church, His people.

You may have seen one of those books that have abstract patterns of colours and shapes. There seems nothing on the page beyond the pretty mix of shades and swirls. But if you de-focus your eyes and stare at the page for a minute or so, out of the mass of colours a hidden shape appears. What looked at first sight to be a random splash of colours is really the Sydney Opera House, or the Eiffel Tower, or some other meaningful picture.

There is a deeper meaning to marriage, a mystery that awaits discovery. Something in marriage unveils the relationship we can have with God through Jesus Christ, and something in your relationship with God in Jesus Christ will help you understand being married.

After quoting Genesis 2:24 in discussing the love of the husband and the wife in marriage, the apostle Paul says: 'This is a profound mystery—but I am talking about Christ and the Church' (Ephesians 5:32, NIV). Another translation puts it this way: 'Marriage is a significant allegory, and I'm applying it to Christ and the church' (CEB). Marriage is a story about another story.

The marriage service places this mystery, or secret, of marriage right up front:

> 'Marriage is the symbol of God's unending love for His people, and of the union between Christ and His Church.' (Marriage AAPB Second Form, 560)

We will better understand the Christian message if we understand the nature of a loving, committed marriage, and we will find insights into the nature of marriage by the light of the Christian message.

Each relationship is a picture of the other.

Love is giving ourselves to the other

As the parties to a marriage give themselves to each other, so in Christ does God give Himself to us, and we respond by the commitment of our lives to God in return. This is the meaning of love: to give ourselves to others, to another (in marriage), and to the Other, our Creator God.

Christianity is about a relationship with God that is very like the kind of loving relationship you find in a healthy, fulfilling marriage. The secret is simple but profound: that marriage is to be *a personal union of lives*, like the Divine-human relationship should be. The apostle Paul explains this resonance between marriage and relationship with God:

> 'That's how husbands ought to love their wives—in the same way as they do their own bodies. Anyone who loves his wife loves himself. No one ever hates his own body, but feeds it and takes care of it just like Christ does for

the church because we are parts of his body. *This is why a man will leave his father and mother and be united with his wife, and the two of them will be one body.* Marriage is a significant allegory, and I'm applying it to Christ and the church. In any case, as for you individually, each one of you should love his wife as himself, and wives should respect their husbands.' (Ephesians 5:28-33, CEB)

Deep and close personal union

Just as the husband and wife become one in a deep personal union, so the believer and the Lord God become one in a union that is real, personal, and loving. The union is to be so close and personal that the interests of the other are regarded as connected to oneself. The two, although still two persons/beings, are joined in a union of lives.

This personal union (husband to wife, believer to the Lord God) is to be a love-union. Let's reflect on what a love-union is like.

The parties unite their lives in love for each other. The two parties, though different, are joined in a union of loving commitment and involvement with each other.

The other person is not to be objectified or used for one's self-oriented benefit.

There is a genuine concern for the other that is planted within the circle of the lover's self. There is mutual giving of self, one to the other.

A good definition of this kind of love—God's kind of love—is found in this description:

> 'Love is that mysterious power by which we live in the lives of others, and are thus moved to benevolent, and even self-sacrificing action on their behalf.' (Robert Law, 75)

This vision of marriage calls us away from all distancing, manipulation, and the selfish self-interest that involves rejection or neglect of the other. There is no place for coercive control in this Divine pattern of relationship and there should be no place for it in marriage.

If you understand what it means to truly love another person in the union of marriage, you will have a big clue about what it means to be loved by God and to love God in return.

The Christian good news and our response to God

In Jesus Christ, God has given Himself to us in sacrifice and personal commitment (Ephesians 5:25). He has identified that our well-being (salvation) is as important to Him as His own Self (Ephesians 5:29).

God does not use coercion to control us but invites, loves, and asks for our love. When we shut Him out of our lives on occasions, by our sins and waywardness, He knocks and asks us to let Him inside to have fellowship with us again (Revelation 3:20).

We respond and give ourselves completely back to God in unreserved, loving commitment.

Marriage is a picture or allegory of the Christian message. Understand marriage as a true love-union, and you will understand what Christianity is about.

Understand the Christian faith as God's giving Himself completely to us, and our complete surrender in love to God, and you will see what marriage is about: a personal relationship that is full, loving, and sacrificial.

Stare at the reality of marriage at its best until you see the beautiful shape of God's love for you forming before your eyes and inviting you to return that love in kind.

Stare at this truth of God's love in its glory until you see the beauty and potential of your marriage-love forming, with new depth in your vision.

In this first section, we have looked at how marriage in God's plan has a design, a foundation on which you can build a good relationship. What materials will you now use to construct your marriage on this design?

A strong marriage will be constructed by fulfilling the vows you make to each other. The next section will focus on these great promises.

Reflection/Discussion: Marriage contains a mystery

1. To understand marriage is to understand the Christian message. What does marriage teach us about God and our relationship with Him?
2. If you understand the Christian gospel, you understand the nature of the marriage union. What does the Christian gospel teach us about how a husband and a wife live together in marriage?

PART 2
CONSTRUCTING A STRONG MARRIAGE

Your marriage is a house built with the strong materials of promise and commitment, expressed in the wedding vows.

8   THE PROMISE TO LOVE

The promise that you will love each other as the marriage moves on in time gives security to the relationship and strengthens your loving, day by day.

In the popular mind and in the movies, the bride and groom say, 'I do.' In the Anglican marriage service, however, they say, 'I will' (Marriage AAPB Second Form, 561).

There is a world of difference between the two responses.

Couples today often want to write their own vows. This is understandable since the wedding is a celebration of their love. The Anglican wedding service vows, however, are more than a *profession* of love; they are *promises* of future commitment in accord with unconditional love.

These traditional vows are not so much *declarations* of present love, as *promises* of future love.

While a couple can make their own personal declarations of love to each other, I believe that it is wise not to replace the Christian vows with romantic, personal versions. The couple can craft their own extra promises if they so desire, and these can be included in the service, whether said at the same time or not. (I think that these personal vows fit well with the exchange of wedding rings.)

Commitment to love in the future

Marriage is a union formed by the love-bond and the marriage-commitment. The marriage service is the occasion for the formal, public, prayerful declaration of the commitment of the couple to love each other in the future.

> 'Will you take N to be your husband/wife, to live together according to God's law? Will you give him/her the honour due to him/her as your husband/wife, and, forsaking all others, love and protect him/her, as long as you both shall live?
> **I will.**' (Marriage AAPB Second Form, 561)

Notice that the couple does not promise that they will stay together 'as long as they both shall *love*'! Rather, they promise to give love to each other as husband and wife, as long as they both shall live. They are pledging to follow a calling; they are entering a vocation—to be married—and to fulfil the duties of that calling.

Listen to Dietrich Bonhoeffer's wise words to his friends on the occasion of their wedding:

> 'Marriage is more than your love for each other ... Your love is your own private possession, but marriage is more than something personal—it is a status, an office. Just as it is the crown, and not merely the will to rule, that makes the king, so it is marriage, and not merely your love for each other, that joins you together in the sight of God and man. As you gave the ring to one another and have now received it a second time from

the hand of the pastor, so love comes from you, but marriage from above, from God. As high as God is above man, so high are the sanctity, the rights, and the promise of marriage above the sanctity, the rights, and the promise of love. It is not your love that sustains the marriage, but from now on, the marriage that sustains the love.' (Bonhoeffer, 1971, 41)

Marriage is built by keeping your promises

The marriage-commitment is the solemn promise to love the other person in the future, to treat the other with the respect and honour that he/she deserves through the new relationship that starts on the wedding day.

The wedding vows can be distilled into three strong promises: (1) To honour (cherish, protect); (2) To be faithful (forsake others, be loyal); and (3) To remain, to stay the course (resilient in commitment).

Your marriage does not depend only on the fuel of your love-bond; it will rely also on your steadfast commitment to love one another even if your love-bond wavers and weakens. The love-bond strengthens the commitment, and the marriage-commitment supports the investment in loving each other. As Bonhoeffer observed: 'It is not your love that sustains the marriage, but from now on, the marriage that sustains the love.'

'Marriage is more than your love for each other,' wrote Bonhoeffer. Your marriage commitment is a choice to continue loving beyond the natural kind of love we have for each other.

Reflection/Discussion: The promise to love

1. 'It is not your love that sustains the marriage, but from now on, the marriage that sustains the love.' Do you agree with Bonhoeffer's statement?
2. What is the difference between the words: 'I do' and 'I will'?

9 TO LOVE, HONOUR, AND PROTECT

You are called to reinforce your marriage-love with the strong promises of honouring and protecting.

What does married love involve? 'Love' is a general, overused word. The marriage service gives shape and colour to the vague word 'love' by attaching other specific actions to it: 'love, comfort, honour, protect' (Marriage APBA Second Order, 660).

Let's consider the commitment to 'honour' one another. To honour someone is to recognise their value and dignity and treat them with respect.

> 'When we honour particular people, we're saying, in effect, that who they are and what they say carries great weight with us. They're extremely valuable in our eyes. Just the opposite is true when we dishonour them. In effect, by our verbal or nonverbal statements we're saying that their words or actions make them of little value or "lightweights" in our eyes.' (Smalley & Trent, 217-8)

Christians are called on to honour God and other people (Revelations 5:12; Romans 12:10). The Bible tells the husband and the wife to honour one another (1 Peter 3:1-7).

What will honouring each other look like in marriage?

We honour each other in marriage when we express in our words and actions the high value and respect we have for each other. The other word used in the wedding vows is 'cherish'. To cherish your spouse is to treat him or her as special and worthy of honour and your best treatment.

Honouring God

We can understand what it means to honour our marriage partner, by looking at the way we should honour God. We offer to our partner an act of adoration and respect that resembles what we offer to God.

We honour God when we worship Him and adore Him, which means giving God His rightful place of importance in our eyes. Honouring our marriage partners likewise means to recognise their value and dignity, and to do so in outward expressions of appreciation and respectful address to them and about them.

The 1662 Anglican marriage service used the word 'worship' in the vows: 'with my body I thee *worship*' (Matrimony BCP, 293). This was the older sense of adore, honour, commit. It is not our way of saying this today, but it captures the reverence, the total commitment of giving oneself to the other, in the physical reality of bodily service.

Honouring means expressing our feelings and responses in a respectful way. Honouring a person does not mean agreeing with them all the time or pretending that their actions and words are blameless when they aren't. Gary Smalley notes: 'Honour is an attitude that someone is valuable. It is not an absolution of all a person's faults, nor a command to be less than honest with who they are' (Smalley & Trent, 227). I think that a synonym would be 'respect'.

We can see what honour involves when we study its opposites: criticism that is destructive in tone and manner; ignoring the other; sarcasm or belittling jokes about the other; rude remarks; making derogatory remarks about your spouse to other people, sometimes in his/her presence.

These kinds of actions convey dishonouring attitudes about the marriage partner. The love-bond of a marriage will be killed by many acts of dishonouring.

The Bible encourages us to give respect and honour to those to whom it is due, because of their responsibilities and roles in relation to us (Romans 13:7). The husband and the wife have received, by their mutual covenant, a calling of special dignity that deserves their mutual respect.

Never forget the respect due to the beloved

The Christian faith offers a powerful insight about how we are to treat each other in marriage. To be a Christian is to be in Christ, with our identity in Him and, through Christ, to others who are also united to Him. Dietrich Bonhoeffer put it like this: 'We belong to one another only through and in Jesus Christ ... A Christian comes to others only through Jesus Christ ... Not what a man is in himself as a Christian, his spirituality and piety, constitutes the basis for our community. What determines our brotherhood is what the man is by reason of Christ' (Bonhoeffer, *Life Together*, 10, 14). We must always give others the honour due to them as people who are with us in Christ.

Just as believers are not to relate to one another 'naturally', forgetting that they are related as brothers and sisters in Christ, and must relate to one another with brotherly/sisterly love through Christ, so the marriage partners must never forget that the other person has a role and status that cannot be disregarded. Husbands and wives should be treated with the respect that their calling deserves.

This is what honouring our spouse means: to treat them with the respect they deserve as the special person with whom we are united in the bond of marriage.

I have been saddened sometimes to see Christian spouses, when their marriage gets into trouble, treating the spouse with less respect or honour than they would give to another fellow Christian brother/sister, or to anyone. We are to honour all people. 'Give respect to those you should respect, and honour those you should honour' (Romans 13:7, CEB).

Honouring and protecting your spouse will go together. We will protect our partner from dangers and harm that threaten their well-being. We will be there for each other. We will protect our marriage.

Reflection/Discussion: To love, honour, and protect

1. How do you 'honour' each other now?
2. What dishonouring attitudes towards each other will you promise to avoid?

10 FORSAKING ALL OTHERS

The Christian marriage commitment is a vow to avoid anyone or anything that gets between you and your beloved spouse.

The marriage commitment is an exclusive commitment; by definition, it draws a boundary around the husband-and-wife bond and warns others to keep out. Jesus said: 'Humans must not pull apart what God has put together' (Matthew 19:6, CEB).

In the marriage service, the wedding couple make a commitment to protect their relationship from involvement with other people in ways that break faith with their spouse:

> 'Will you ... forsaking all others, be faithful to him/her, as long as you both shall live?' (Marriage AAPB First Form, 548)

This warning recognises that there may be others who will try to separate the couple by interference, jealousy, or seduction. Spouses, too, might pull apart their own bond by unfaithfulness or abuse.

The marriage commitment is a promise to be faithful and not to commit adultery in body or heart, expressing the intention to obey the seventh commandment of God: 'Do not commit adultery' (Exodus 20:14, CEB).

You promise to protect the marriage

The thought of being unfaithful to one's marriage partner will not normally be in the minds of the couple at their wedding. It should not be a hard commitment for most marrying couples to make on their wedding day. In time, however, it may become a hard commitment to maintain.

The Anglican *Book of Common Prayer* marriage service contains a memorable way of expressing this resolution: 'and thereto I plight thee my troth' (Matrimony BCP, 293). 'Troth' is one of those archaic words that captures a range of helpful nuances. Troth is close in meaning, as in spelling, to the word 'truth'. It means being 'true', trustworthy, having integrity, and showing faithfulness. To give someone your promise of *troth* is to assure him or her that they can rely on you, that you will be devoted and loyal to them.

Marriage is a commitment to be '*trothful*', which will mean being *truthful*, and truthfulness is essential to faithfulness. Adultery is a dishonest action and is hidden until it is discovered. It is built on lies. The Christian way of relationships, in marriage and in other settings, is '*speaking the truth with love*' (Ephesians 4:15, CEB).

Infidelity in marriage is usually a sign that there is a problem in the relationship, for one or both partners. In an 'affair', part of the real person has been withdrawn from the marriage and entrusted to someone else. There is a failure to be close and connected with your spouse, and a failure of integrity to deal truthfully in keeping your promises.

Jesus Christ deepened this issue by pointing out how adultery can be committed in the heart and mind, apart from sexual or physical involvement:

> 'You have heard that it was said: *Don't commit adultery.* But I say to you that every man who looks at a woman lustfully has already committed adultery in his heart.'
> (Matthew 5:27-28, CEB)

Your marriage commitment is your promise to put a boundary up against improper involvement with a rival to your spouse.

The Christian's exclusive allegiance to the Lord

This commitment to be loyal and not allow another to come between you and your spouse is like the Christian's commitment of faithfulness to the Lord God. The relationship between the Lord God and His people is likened in the Bible to a kind of marriage, and there is constant danger that the people-partner will be lured away in their hearts and lives by other allegiances and commit spiritual adultery.

In the Bible, the allegiance of the people of God to their Lord will mean that they do not put some other god in His place. 'Little children, guard yourselves from idols!' (1 John 5:21, CEB). Idolatry is likened to adultery.

Just as the disciple is to allow no one to take God's place in his/her life (Exodus 20:3), so the Christian spouse recognises that there is a loyalty in heart and life owed to one's spouse that must not be given to anyone else.

In the baptism service, the new disciple turns to Christ and away from the world and all that competes with God:

> 'Do you renounce the devil and all his works, the empty display and false values of the world, and the sinful desires of the flesh, so that you will not follow

nor be led by them?' (Infant Baptism AAPB First Form, 502)

In the marriage service, each party makes a renunciation of alternative heart-allegiances to other people and pursuits that may take the place of the spouse in their lives.

This loyalty will involve more than avoiding adultery. It will be a positive allegiance of heart, mind, will, and body.

Reflection/Discussion: Forsaking all others

1. What boundaries will you both set to protect your marriage from improper bonding with others?
2. Infidelity often happens when a marriage relationship is impoverished, and one or both partners in the marriage are withholding their real selves from each other. How can you avoid withdrawing your *self* from the marriage?

11 BE FAITHFUL TO YOUR SPOUSE

Faithfulness to one another calls for active, aware involvement, and the same applies to being faithful to our God.

You promise to be faithful to your spouse in the Christian marriage service (Marriage AAPB First Form, 548). Being faithful involves more than just avoiding adultery.

This strong commitment will demand your active energy to fulfil it. It is designed to protect your marriage. By making a clear commitment to be reliable and faithful, you invite your partner to count on you. By being trustworthy, you both establish a cycle of increasing trust, understanding, and love.

Think of trust in your marriage as like a bank deposit. You both begin your married life by making a public donation of trust into each other's heart. Before God and others, you state publicly that you will be faithful to each other—and then you sign a legal document to that effect! You are inviting every witness (including God) to hold you accountable for keeping your promises.

Already, in your relationship before marriage, you have

been building your trust in each other. Keeping this promise is much more than avoiding adultery. To be faithful means keeping your commitments consistently, and in many little things.

Your character is behind this promise. How special will you make your spouse in your life? Will he or she know constantly that you are cherishing his or her special place in your heart?

How do we keep this promise, to be faithful only to our marriage partner? The spiritual parallel once again is helpful.

Faithfulness in the Christian life

There are clues in the Christian faith about what marital faithfulness should look like. The Christian already has some experience of what faithfulness is like.

We have a God who is faithful to His promises, who can be relied on to be trustworthy (1 Thessalonians 5:24). In the marriage commitment to be faithful to your beloved, you are imitating the Lord who is the faithful God who commits Himself to us and can be counted on, who promises His people: '*I will never leave you or abandon you*' (Hebrews 13:5, CEB). We are to be like the faithful God we serve, and to be reliable and trustworthy. We are to be faithful to other people in the fellowship of Christ, as well as being faithful to our Lord (Galatians 5:22).

The Christian who is getting married also knows about the calling to be faithful in the sphere of his or her relationship with God. The concept of faith in God is essentially *faithfulness* to God—loyalty or allegiance to God.

Faith is much more than belief in your head and heart; it is allegiance. It is seen in outward evidence of loyalty (Bates, 68, 154).

Faithfulness will be seen in public. The Christian service of baptism marks this public act of commitment to be faithful in allegiance:

> 'I sign you with the sign of the cross, to show that you are to be true to Christ crucified, and that you are not to be ashamed to confess your faith in Him. Fight bravely under His banner, against sin, the world, and the devil, and continue Christ's faithful soldier and servant to your life's end.' (Public Baptism of Infants AAPB Second Order, 523)

In the baptism service, the new Christian is welcomed into the congregation and signed with the sign of the cross to indicate the calling 'to continue Christ's faithful soldier and servant to your life's end' (Adult Baptism AAPB First Order, 510).

Faithfulness—tested by temptations

We also know that faithfulness will be tested. We know that staying faithful to God will involve challenges, from within and from outside. This lesson is basic to the Christian life: *'keep us from being tempted and protect us from evil'* (Matthew 6:13, CEV). The Christian knows that there are many temptations around us that lure us away from faithful love for God. You will need to watch for the traps or snares that will spoil your spiritual relationship with God.

The same danger confronts your marriage. It is naive to ignore this risk to your vows.

To keep the marriage commitment, we must also learn to recognise the danger signs. Infidelity begins in the heart and mind (Matthew 5:27-30). Walter Wangerin warns about the early signs of a temptation to unfaithfulness:

> 'Adultery is never a sudden, spontaneous, and totally unexpected act ... Early on in extramarital friendship, there often comes a moment of "maybe" ... A mutual understanding seems to establish itself between you, unspoken ... This is the moment of "maybe".' (Wangerin, 196)

There are vulnerable times when temptation comes. Christian spouses should know about the principles of dealing with temptations. It is one thing to *feel* an inappropriate attraction, but another to *feed* an attraction.

Invest in your relationship

The Christian learns that a proactive approach will be necessary. You will need to invest in your relationship with God and keep moving closer to the Lord (Philippians 3:12-16).

In a healthy Christian life, the believer is constantly investing in his/her relationship with the Lord. We follow our Lord by actively staying connected to Him, listening to His commands, and drawing life from our relationship with God. Jesus says to His people:

> 'Remain in me, and I will remain in you. A branch can't produce fruit by itself but must remain in the vine. Likewise, you can't produce fruit unless you remain in me ... Remain in my love. If you keep my commandments, you will remain in my love, just as I kept my Father's commandments and remain in His love.' (John 15:4, 9-10, CEB)

Faithfulness to one another in the marriage relationship will follow a similar pattern to our Christian life.

Let the husband and wife continually invest in their relationship, putting each other in that special place in their hearts and lives, and cherishing their relationship. Stay connected to each other in active ways. Being faithful is an active challenge.

The Christian marriage partner will not treat a temptation to be unfaithful as anything less than a danger.

Reflection/Discussion: Be faithful to your spouse

1. What are the danger signs of potential infidelity?
2. What lessons about being faithful to God can help you be faithful to your marriage partner?

12 A LIFELONG UNION

Your marriage must be prepared to face the ups and downs of life in a lifetime commitment.

Years ago, I was shocked by a comment of a Christian woman, as she reflected about how her marriage had ended, saying that 'he was a good first husband'. I don't know if she intentionally went into that union with this view or looking back at how she or they had changed along the way, she saw that they were not ready for a lasting relationship.

It is difficult to imagine how a total love-commitment of a whole life to another could be offered on any other basis than 'until death parts us'. This is the intention, although many marriages do not last that long, failing through sinful choices or weaknesses, neglect, or a gradual ceasing to care or to desire to make it work. The biblical phrase calls this 'hardness of heart'.

The Anglican marriage service declares: 'Scripture teaches that marriage is a lifelong partnership uniting a woman and a man in heart, mind and body' (Marriage APBA Second Order, 658).

The Christian way of marriage sees it as a 'whole-life

commitment': a 'whole-person' commitment, for a 'whole lifetime'.

Lifetime commitments

There is a challenge in making a major life-commitment. Can we make it now for all the years that may lie ahead, when so much of the future is unknown?

What if I or we change? In fact, this is what happens for all of us; we change as the years move forward. We may marry as young adults, but as we reach middle age we are looking at life differently, and perhaps issues that were buried in our hearts have begun to bubble up and disturb the surface of our lives and relationships. I have seen this in my pastoral ministry. Some problems in marriages come from personal, buried issues, which were out of sight when the youthful vows were taken.

Realism about the future

The Christian way of marriage realistically acknowledges this fact of change over time. Your marriage commitment envisages a lifelong partnership of growth in love and friendship through a variety of experiences. The wedding service includes this realistic comment:

> 'In the joys and sorrows of life, in prosperity and adversity, they share their companionship, faithfulness and strength.' (Marriage APBA Second Form, 560)

This extensive, enduring commitment calls for thoughtful realism, and readiness to make it work all the way to the end. The marriage service and its vows recognise the challenge of a lifelong commitment.

It is certainly true, sadly, that couples can grow *away from* each other as they change. We must recognise that we will need to seek to grow *closer to* each other as we grow older and change.

A lifelong commitment brings challenges to stay the distance and finish well.

What should we realistically expect is ahead of your marriage as it moves on for a lifetime together?

Lifelong commitments: marriage and following the Lord

The marriage vows are realistic about the challenges that lie ahead. The vows are unconditional, envisaging all kinds of good and bad as part of the married couple's experience. The couple promises to stay together whatever the circumstances. This is easy to say before the challenges come along.

The Christian knows that following the Lord Jesus is also a lifetime commitment—a 'forever' decision. God has made an eternal promise to us: 'I will never leave you or abandon you' (Hebrews 13:5, CEB). We respond accordingly to 'continue Christ's faithful soldier and servant to [our] life's end' (Adult Baptism AAPB Second Form, 531).

When we think of some of the challenges to a lifelong marriage commitment, it is good to look to the wisdom of the Christian faith, with its insights about making and keeping lifetime commitments.

Here are three challenges to making lifetime commitments, in marriage and in faith.

1. Fading idealism

The promise to love can seem naturally easy at the start but may become difficult in time. There is a lot of hope and idealism at the start. It is good, then, that the words of the wedding vows ('for better, for worse') sound a realistic note amidst the glamour and fantasy of a wedding ceremony.

The Christian life also often starts out with a youthful idealism about the challenges of a lifelong, whole-life commitment to the Lord.

The baptism service, like the marriage service, sounds a realistic note. The newly baptised believer is encouraged to remain Christ's faithful soldier and servant until his/her life's end (Baptism AAPB First Order, 510). Obedience to God is a long-distance race, and there will be some hills and bad weather along the route. This will mean coping with all 'the changes and chances of this fleeting world' (as the Anglican liturgy describes life).

You dedicate your life to the Lord Jesus Christ *before* you learn how hard it will be to fulfil your calling. You join your lives as a married couple together (usually) *before* you encounter the trials of life that put a strain on your love and commitment.

2. Suffering and difficulties

Your marriage commitment recognises the sufferings that are likely to arise during such a long relationship. There will be crises and difficulties between the wedding day and the golden wedding anniversary, and couples who make the distance are to be congratulated.

Here is another similarity with the Christian life. Christian disciples know that following Christ, while it brings wonderful joys, calls for constant changes and a willingness to endure for His sake.

Of all the people who marry, Christians should understand that a long-term relationship will have its costs as well as its joys, its troubles as well as its triumphs.

The Christian life can start off with strong love for God, but time, troubles, and temptations can drain away youthful, early love for Christ (Revelation 2:4). How many believers fall away when the going gets tough or temptations besiege the heart!

We speak of our married love like this sometimes. We say that the flame of love has gone out; how can we rekindle our love?

The Christian faith has wisdom for this business of maintaining lifelong commitments. Those who follow Christ must learn that they need to work on keeping their faith '*on fire in the Spirit*' (Romans 12:11, CEB).

3. Changes in yourself, your partner, and your marriage

Your marriage commitment is to a real person, who will change as the years roll on. You yourself will change.

To live is to change. The couple may live together through their youth, the crowded years of parenting and careers, their middle age, the empty nest when children have left, and then increasing health problems of aging.

Life-crises may load serious strains on their marriage-bond. This is when the commitment we make—to love *this* particular person in all the changes and chances of life—makes a huge difference.

In my pastoral ministry, I have observed that many men seem to encounter a mid-life emotional transition. As they move past their midway point of life, they sometimes get unsettled and decide to change careers or other aspects of their life.

Life, including marriage and family, seems unsatisfying. I have talked often to young couples about this as they prepare for marriage. The bride needs to be ready, and the groom as well, for the inner personal changes that they may both encounter as they grow older together. Women, too, face similar challenges of life-changes in body and emotions.

Marriages have stages

Your marriage commitment for lifetime union should include awareness of needing to adapt to the stages of married life.

Just as married partners can change as life proceeds, so too marriages develop and change through stages. It is wise to recognise that your marriage will change, and you must cope with these transitions.

James Greteman has listed five stages:

1. the romantic stage
2. the power stage, when differences become a challenge
3. the stability stage, when differences are sorted out satisfactorily
4. the commitment stage, when they live on the basis of their union
5. the 'co-creation' stage, when the fruit of the marriage is enjoyed. (Greteman, 13-18)

The spiritual life has its changes and stages

The Christian life, too, has its stages of growth (1 John 2:12-14).

We begin as babies, infants in faith. We grow to young adulthood and start learning lessons of challenge and spiritual warfare. Hopefully, we learn, in the school of prayer and obedience, lessons of wisdom from God.

Some give up their faith when they are only just experiencing the need to grow beyond a child's level of understanding. Some fail to realise that the way of Christian maturity follows the road of obedience and hard experience. In the memorable picture that Jesus gave, we need to be like wise builders who build on bedrock, so that when the rains fall, the floods come, and the wind blows and beats upon our lives, we will stand firm (Matthew 7:24-27). As in the Christian life, so in the way of Christian marriage, it is vital to build on solid foundations with strong materials of love and commitment.

The calling to be married, like the calling to follow Christ, is a calling to face changes and challenges, and to grow together. However we understand the stages of a marriage's life, it is obvious that a couple must be prepared to adapt together and work on sustaining a growing, mutually satisfying relationship in all the varied experiences of a lifetime.

Your marriage will change. Work together on your marriage, as you change together in marriage.

We have considered God's design for your marriage, and the shape of your commitment to love each other. This commitment is like the internal structure of your house, the load-bearing walls of your vows that give room for your love to grow and flourish.

You build the walls of your marriage with the strong materials of your promises to be faithful, to honour, and to cherish each other, and to stay the course in all the ups and downs of life and its changes.

Then you start to live in your 'house' of marriage. How will you organise it and live together? What are your respective roles? In the next chapter we come down to earth from the romantic idealism of the wedding and honeymoon and think about the day-to-day practicalities of two living as one.

Reflection/Discussion: A lifelong union

1. Think about how you will both sustain a commitment that may last your whole lives. How will you renew and renegotiate this commitment, to keep it strong?

2. List some possible challenges you may face in your marriage. How prepared are you to overcome them, together?

PART 3
ORGANISING YOUR MARRIED LIFE TOGETHER

How does a Christian couple, or any couple, work together in their joint task of building their marriage and their home?

13 YOUR MARRIAGE IS A SPECIAL KIND OF FRIENDSHIP

Marriage is more than just friendship, but it is not less than friendship. It is made up of the disciplines or habits that make a good friendship.

The marrying couple makes a commitment to be faithful friends, companions, to each other. Marriage is a covenant of companionship.

> 'In the joys and sorrows of life, in prosperity and adversity, they share their companionship, faithfulness and strength.' (Marriage APBA Second Form, 560)

You promise to live together in a lifetime of companionship. To build a successful marriage, the husband and wife need to build a strong friendship.

Couples who have moved in together before they formally take their wedding vows have already started their friendship in close quarters, with the everyday issues of sharing a home. But marriage is a friendship, a companionship to last a lifetime, so it is worth more reflection.

It is well to understand what friendship will require from

both of you. There are laws of friendship—principles that make companionship work.

Becoming good companions

Alan Craddock affirms the importance of building a good marriage friendship as life-companions, based on the extensive research of the *Prepare* Pre-Marriage Inventory:

> 'Good marriages are based on good companionship. Happy married couples like being together and talking to one another. They pursue dreams together and gain strength from making plans and facing challenges. They do not argue and bicker continually and they work as a unit. This requires effort, but it is effort which ensures a rich reward for those who make it work.' (Craddock, 26)

What makes a good companionship? I think it is obvious that there needs to be shared values and goals. Beyond this similarity of outlook, companionship requires good communication, effective conflict resolution, and a cooperative attitude.

We can call these the three Cs of married companionship: Communication, Constructive Conflict, and Cooperation.

Communication: listening and talking

Good communication is vital to an effective, fulfilling marriage. Research has shown what type of communication works in marriage: listening very carefully and non-judgmentally to each other; talking and discussing with each other; understanding without words; and encouragement through affirmation and appreciation (Craddock, 5-7).

Counsellors know that active listening and good communication do not come naturally to most of us and demand skills that need to be learned and practised. It may be helpful for the engaged couple to do some training in listening and communication skills, such as *Effectiveness Training* or similar courses in Active Listening (Gordon, 1975).

The importance of good communication skills was demonstrated right in front of me years ago, when an engaged couple came to see me because they were having conflict in their relationship. As they talked in my office, an argument erupted, with a good deal of emotion in the exchanges.

When they paused their interaction, I asked them if I could explain what I saw happening in their communication. I explained how they were not listening or communicating effectively. I shared with them some different, more constructive ways of communicating, and then I asked them to have the argument again—this time using a different approach. They were amazed at the contrast.

We met together over several weeks as they practised key effective-communication skills at home. Good communication skills can save a marriage.

Constructive conflict resolution

Married companions will have conflicts: the issue is how they are handled. 'Unless a couple have learned successful ways of handling these [conflict] situations the conflict can become destructive and communication then becomes closed-off and hostile,' notes Alan Craddock (Craddock, 7).

How we resolve our conflicts is a crucial skill for a good marriage. Each of us grew up learning some lessons about conflict and how it was handled—or mishandled. These conflict 'styles' may be quite unhelpful, but they are programmed into our personalities. A successful marriage must learn how to disagree and resolve conflicts in a constructive way. We will look at this in Chapter 24.

Cooperative attitude

The two learn to act as one. The two find a new unity in action and will. They bring an attitude of cooperation and mutual adjustment to their relationship, and it bears fruit in harmony. The words of Jesus about marriage, that they are no longer two, but one, have many daily applications for the couple. They must think of the 'we' as much as the 'me'.

Companionship with God

Those who want a Christian marriage—a marriage in which the Lord is a real participant in the relationship—can find some insights about married friendship from their Christian 'friendship' with God.

Learning to *listen to God* is a lifetime challenge for the disciple. *Waiting* on God is a Christian way of describing the attitude of receptive attention to what God is saying to us. We also will have our disagreements or issues with God, which we need to bring to the Lord in honesty. The Bible has a lot of honest prayers, where the believer is in pain and perplexity and lays it out before the Lord. Prayer is communication with God, speaking as well as listening.

There are various 'spiritual disciplines', such as prayer, meditation, Bible study and other practices, that help us develop our relationship with God (Willard, 2012; Ford, 2008).

As listening to God requires an alert and attentive heart to know God's will, so the married Christian must work at learning to listen to the married partner attentively. Communication takes time and attention. In the busyness of life, sometimes we stop setting aside dedicated time to listen to and talk with each other. Christians allocate time to focus attention on God (worship, prayer), and to be together, giving and receiving. A relationship with God that has no designated time for focused attention will stagnate.

In the early days of my marriage, this was a hard lesson for me to learn as a young husband. I was preoccupied with my work and studies, and my wife was finding her job challenging. Life was settling into a rut, and I found out to my dismay that she was not enjoying married life, feeling that I was not listening to her. It was a big wake-up call to me as a husband. So, we resolved to have an evening dedicated to communicating with each other—a weekly time to just be together without other concerns or distractions intruding. In the decades since, we have kept up the habit of making time to communicate, and just be together.

Cooperating with God

To cooperate with God is central to following Christ. We must learn to submit our self-will to God and to work in cooperation with His purposes, which we now identify as ours too. The Christian knows that this adjusting our will to God's will is an ongoing challenge. This is why we pray it daily in the Lord's Prayer: 'Your will be done.'

Just as the Christian wants to join his/her will to God's will, so the married couple will want to have a unity of wills in a cooperative way. Christian spouses will work on joining their wills together.

Just as the Christian wants to pursue God's will beyond one's own will, the married couple will seek to find a higher purpose together that enables them to work together as one.

Surely such a higher, ruling purpose or 'will' is the couple's calling to become one and build a successful friendship. This may call for a lot of little surrenders from each, and much careful communication to find their united way forward.

To be a faithful companion in marriage is to be committed to do what it takes to maintain and strengthen the friendship.

This cannot be taken for granted. Communication can be challenging, conflict resolution is sometimes demanding, and developing a cooperative attitude requires a struggle with our natural selfishness.

The Christian knows that the spiritual life with God is a challenge to become closer to the Lord in companionship and in alignment of our will. Married friendship will also be a growing companionship.

Reflection/Discussion: Your marriage is a special kind of friendship

1. Your lifelong 'companionship' will need to be strong in communication, conflict resolution and cooperation. How strong are you now in these three areas?
2. Resolve now to improve your skills in communication. Enrol in a course or find someone to teach you more about effective listening and constructive conflict resolution.

14 MARRIAGE ROLES

Is there a set of defined roles for husbands and wives in a Christian marriage?

How will you organise your life together in your 'house' of marriage? What roles will the husband and wife follow in the marriage relationship? Is there a 'job description' for a Christian husband and a Christian wife?

The Christian husband and wife are called to a deep oneness of life and love; they are joint heirs of the grace of life, says the apostle Peter (1 Peter 3:7). How does this unity work out in practice? How is the marriage relationship organised in everyday life? Who does what? Does the Bible set down a permanent set of rules for roles in marriage?

Some of the biblical passages set for weddings seem to lay out a specific kind of relationship structure for marriage. In one of the classic biblical passages about marriage, the apostle Paul says: 'wives, submit to your husbands as to the Lord, for the husband is the head of the wife as Christ is the head of the Church' (Ephesians 5:22-23, HCSB). These words are out of step with modern egalitarian views on marriage. What do they mean for us? Is this some out-of-date concept, or even a dangerous idea?

Christian people have different views about how to interpret and apply the biblical passages about the marriage relationship. In this and the next chapter we will consider two main options: the traditional view (applying the Bible passages directly), and the alternative, egalitarian interpretation (applying the biblical text with some cultural adjustment).

As with the question of divorce and remarriage, we face here an issue where sincere Christians disagree, and which poses questions about our interpretation and application of the Bible. The matter is complex, but it is important that a couple work out together how they will relate together in a satisfactory way for both, and as Christians how they will be of one mind about God's will for their relating. Whether the couple opts to follow a traditional or an egalitarian pattern of marriage roles, it is vital that they agree about what it will mean in practice.

Let's consider a traditional way of reading the Bible's instructions to husbands and wives (for example, Paul in Ephesians 5:21-33, Colossians 3:18, and Titus 2:3-6). When the Bible writers urged wives to submit to their husbands, what did they have in mind? What exactly was this headship of the husband?

Marriage structure in biblical days

We must see these biblical instructions in their own context to appreciate their force. The New Testament writers were addressing a traditional social culture and applying the good news of Christ to the marriage structures and laws of their day. There were hierarchies in society and in the family. The husband was the head of the household; he was the head of his wife. There was an authority role for the husband in Roman law; the wife was subordinate, and her role was to submit to her husband's authority. Marriage roles were also changing too, as a new type of 'Roman woman' was emerging, more liberated and assertive in financial and sexual freedoms (Winter, 22ff). Emperor Augustus had issued new legislation in 17 BC aimed at strengthening the moral faithfulness of spouses (Winter, 18, 42). The cultural situation on Crete, addressed by Paul through Titus, had its own specific issues in marriage and sexual morality. It is possible that Paul's injunctions to the young Christian Cretan wives to be submissive to their husbands (Titus 2:3-6) was responding to behaviour that was following newer secular trends of sexual liberation and irresponsibility. Bruce Winter suggests: 'The neglect of her husband as well as her children presumably in favour of a social life that might involve casual extramarital affairs is also commented on' (Winter, 168). Christian women were in danger of following the wrong pattern of married life and thereby bringing the Christian way of marriage and the faith into disrepute.

This was the world that the biblical writers addressed. How did they respond to it? They accepted the social conservatism of their society but began to change it.

We can detect in the New Testament writings that the Christian message was beginning to transform the marriage and family patterns of church members. The marriage structure that recognised the authority of the husband as head, and the wife's subordination to her husband, was not overthrown, but it was to be changed significantly. There was both continuity and change in marriage norms for these first Christians. As their faith was applied in marriage, they began to redefine the way that headship and submission were practised.

The *Christian* husband's headship or leadership was now to be sacrificial, loving, modelled on Christ's self-giving love for the Church, His bride. The *Christian* wife's response to her husband's leadership was now to be like her response to her Lord—willing, joyful, loving, and cooperative. The behaviour of both men and women in the church must not bring discredit on the message of the good news of Christ.

The ancient cultural pattern of marriage was being adapted in the early church to reflect the unity of love and mutual care that marks the Christian vision of relationships in Christ. This was a radical transformation of the ancient pattern of marriage. The outward structure of roles was kept, but the motivation was new. The surrounding ancient marriage culture believed in the husband's headship and the wife's submission, but the Christian church poured into this structure the new wine of grace, sacrifice, and love.

As modern people in the egalitarian West, we miss the radical nature of the apostle Paul's instructions in Ephesians 5. 'Wives, submit to your own husbands as you do to the Lord' (Ephesians 5:22, NIV) shocks us, but we need to understand 'that for the first century audience it was not the wife material that was radical or strange; it was the husband material' (Webb, 80). The husband's rule or authority was understood, but the command to husbands to love their wives as Christ loved the Church and gave himself up for her to make her holy (Ephesians 5:25) was shockingly radical.

We must hear the Bible's words about 'headship' and 'submission' with Christian, New Testament ears; these are good, blessed concepts. The Son, Jesus, submitted to God the Father; the disciple willingly submits to the Lord; the headship of the Lord Jesus is a saving, protecting care.

The apostle Paul did not give a theological foundation for authority and submission in marriage, just guidance that the couple work out their marriage relationship as is appropriate in the Lord, showing the way of love and self-giving in their roles (Colossians 3:18).

Headship and submission today?

To the Christian couple who believes that there is a biblical directive to adopt the marriage structure of the husband's headship and the wife's subordination, here are some important angles to consider:

1. Talk over what you both think this will involve, and make sure that you have agreement about how you want your roles to work. There are many couples who have successful marriages with this role structure, but it should be mutual and a blessing.
2. Recognise that the Bible does not give specific job descriptions or roles to the husband and wife. The details of what headship involves or what submission entails are not specified. We should be careful of imposing an invented legalism on the Christian way of marriage. Just adopting this theological structure for your marriage roles does not solve the practical issues of living together. The Bible does not give us rules and cases for how the marriage roles work out. This is not the way that the biblical material works. There usually are principles and we work out the applications in love and wisdom. I have found that some Christian books about the headship and submission model end up in a legalistic mess of trying to work out specifics. They certainly go beyond the instructions of the Bible.
3. If a couple wants to adopt a traditional pattern of the husband's headship and the wife's subordination, they need to realise that such a marriage should be filled with the sacrificial love modelled by Christ and the love of mutual

submission of each other (Ephesians 5:21). I believe that it is possible for a Christian couple to believe in a traditional-type headship and submission idea of marriage, while in practice operating in a respectful, cooperative and functionally egalitarian way. Giving up oneself *for* the other and giving up oneself *to* the other may end up being very similar, and hard to tell apart.
4. Be aware that there is a potential danger that may lurk behind this view. For the man who wants to dominate his wife, this theology of 'headship' is a great cover and justification. He may even sincerely believe that this is his calling from God.

A proposal for spiritual headship

I believe that there may be a continuing relevant application of the traditional model of marriage in our different culture. There may still be a principle of marriage order here that transcends the original cultural context.

Is it possible that there may be a headship-submission structure in a Christian marriage that does not involve power, patriarchy, or female subordination? I think there may be an application that is relevant today.

Here is my suggested continuing spiritual principle that may still apply to our day. The key is found in the fact that the relationship on view may be spiritual, and not relating to authority or decision-making at all.

The clue is found in the relationship of the Lord Jesus Christ to the believer. The husband's headship is to be like Christ's, exercised by the husband for the sake of his wife. Christ's headship is defined as His victory over the powers of evil for the sake of the Church (Ephesians 1:22-23). He leads, nurtures, and protects the Church (Ephesians 1:17-23; 5:23, 25-30).

The husband's headship as a Christian now does not necessarily mean only, or mainly, formal authority. There is an aspect of headship, seen in Christ, that is still very good: protection, including spiritual protection. Christ's headship was for the Church, exercised on our behalf, for our sakes. He got between the powers of evil and the Church, defeating them at great cost to Himself.

In the natural order of family and marriage, we often see this protective role of the husband/father. When his wife and family are in danger, the husband-father will act instinctively to protect them, even at the cost of his life. We saw this happen dramatically in the tragic massacre at Port Arthur in Tasmania years ago. The men immediately put themselves between the bullets and their families.

The husband's particular responsibility in marriage is similar: to provide nurturing love to his wife, to give spiritual leadership in the family, and to protect his wife in the spiritual warfare, as he walks in the Spirit with the Lord as his strength (Ephesians 6:10-20).

There is a hint of this kind of husbandly headship in 1 Corinthians 11:10. The husband is called to put up a spiritual umbrella of prayer, holiness, and protection over his wife and family.

We know that there is a protective role for the husband/father in marriage and family. Headship once contained authority as well as protection and nurture. In an egalitarian marriage the authority element from traditional customs has become obsolete for many. The spiritual headship of sacrificial care and protection may still be relevant and blessed.

The Christian husband is called to exercise a *spiritual* leadership which is different to a governing or ruling authority.

I am not suggesting that the wife has no responsibility for spiritual protection in the marriage and the family. The woman, too, will give up her life for her family in danger and in times of need. She will give herself to those she loves and serves. Her spiritual submission as to the Lord is not servile obedience to her husband, but her willing unity with him in service, like her willing service for the Lord.

Submission is also a mutual obligation for Christians (Ephesians 5:21). Everyone lives under someone's headship in different spheres of life. We are to be ready to give way to others for the sake of the good and blessing of all.

Let the Christian husband realise he is called to a spiritually protective role for his wife and family. Having a serving, loving spiritual protector will be a blessing for the wife.

In the next chapter, we will look at the egalitarian way of Christian marriage.

Reflection/Discussion: Marriage roles

1. What view of the roles of husband and wife do you each hold—traditional or egalitarian, or another view? Do you agree with each other?
2. What do you think of the idea that the husband's headship in Christian marriage is a spiritual leadership role marked by prayer, holiness, love, and protection?

15 KEEPING GOD'S COMMANDS IN A DIFFERENT ERA

How do we express in our different culture the spirit of a biblical, Christian marriage?

'The concept of marriage between equal partners is just beginning to be perceived in the New Testament', wrote I. Howard Marshall, 'and Paul should not be expected to step outside his time and see the consequences of his teaching' (Pierce, Groothuis & Fee, 195). Just as the New Testament writers were applying the good news of Christ to the specific marriage customs of their day, so we must do the same, and put the gospel to work in a new day.

In the previous study, we noted that the New Testament passages on marriage come from a cultural context marked by definite role and power differences between husbands and wives, men and women. These New Testament biblical instructions were given to adapt the practice of marriage in that day to the values of the Christian way. The husbands in that culture were the head of the household—let them be loving, sacrificial leaders in their role. Wives in those days were expected to submit to the authority and leadership of their husband—let them do so in willing, gracious love.

Our contemporary Western marriage context

We know that there have been vast changes in how men and women relate together in our modern Western society, and that even the concept of marriage has been cut loose from its biological sexual complementarity for reproduction. Many see the Bible's notion of marriage as an old, outdated idea. I have argued that the one-flesh union for reproduction and family is not superseded now; it is a natural and creaturely reality. However, there are some cultural aspects that may not be central to the marriage union and may differ across time and cultures. The issue of authority and roles needs to be approached carefully.

Our contemporary cultural setting of marriage is now very different. The modern Church in our Western society lives in a day when egalitarian marriages are the norm.

How do we apply the Bible's teaching to our marriages? We can understand that the New Testament was applying the spirit of the good news to the structures of ancient marriage culture. What persists to our day for us to follow?

Marriage: the structure and the spirit

I believe that we must interpret the New Testament guidance on marriage with adjustment to our different cultural context. We do not need to keep the cultural form of marriage from the first century, with its authority structure. I do not think that we get a law or prescription about marriage *roles* in the Scriptures. But I do believe that we have clear guidance about marriage *motivation* in the Bible.

In this issue of marriage, we face an application challenge similar to many other biblical examples. Biblical commands were given in a particular cultural situation. The principle of the command was to find expression in a culturally appropriate way. In case after case, the reader of the Bible must discern what is the principle that transcends the original biblical expression. William J. Webb distinguishes the 'cultural component' (which may be superseded) from the 'transcultural component', the timeless truths relevant today in different cultural settings (Webb, 24).

I call these two aspects the *structure* and the *spirit*. There is the traditional marriage roles of headship and submission (the structure), and the Christian call to love and sacrifice (the spirit). The structure was the first-century Roman Mediterranean marriage law and custom; the spirit is the biblical calling to love, give, and sacrifice.

Some Christians insist that the ancient marriage structure is still the God-given, revealed pattern of marriage: the husband is the authoritative head, and the wife is to submit, but with the new life of the gospel directing the way it works for both. Other Christians believe that the headship and submission pattern is not essential to their marriages today; it was part of the now-obsolete cultural marriage structure.

Whatever marriage *structure* you follow, the call to love, service, and sacrifice—the *spirit* of Christ—applies to us, as much as it did to the first generation of Christians.

Similar Bible application issues

So we have two elements in these New Testament texts, which I have called the *structure* and the *spirit*. The *structure* is the headship of the husband; the *spirit* is the sacrificial, self-giving love of the husband as head. The *structure* is the wife's submission; the *spirit* is her willing submission of herself to her husband, as part of her service to her Lord Jesus.

We face a similar question elsewhere in applying the Bible to our situations. We must apply the Christian precepts and principles in different social contexts. My view is that the cultural context of our obedience does shape the form it takes. Literal application is not always required for faithfulness to scriptural principles. Most Christians do this already in other areas, although some can hold onto literal applications.

Here are some examples. We can greet one another in love without the 'kiss' that the apostle commanded (1 Peter 5:14; 1 Thessalonians 5:26). The call to welcome each other abides; the *holy kiss* is cultural.

In the first century Graeco-Roman culture it was expected that women would cover their heads in public and some other settings; veiling was a cultural norm. In our Australian and Western society, married Christian women usually do not have to veil their heads to be culturally appropriate (1 Corinthians 11:1-16). Proper conduct and modesty of dress is the principle; the head covering is cultural.

In our church practice, we usually understand that the *principle* can be kept, while the *expression* of the principle may be culturally conditioned. The *principle* (proper attitude towards husbands and society) abides; the *expression* of the principle may vary.

I conclude that obedience to Scripture then does not necessarily require us to replicate or maintain the patriarchal marriage and family life appropriate in the ancient Mediterranean world of the first century.

Faithfulness to Christ may be expressed in modern marriages somewhat differently, since this is a vastly different world—a world where women are educated and filling leadership roles, which was unusual in biblical times.

Reflection/Discussion: Keeping God's commands in a different era

1. Do you agree that applying the principle of a

biblical text sometimes means a different expression culturally? Discuss.
2. How do you envisage mutual submission as Christians will work out in the marriage you want to form, whether traditional or egalitarian?

16 THE WIFE AND HER HUSBAND

Just as the believer aligns his or her will with the Lord Jesus, so the Christian wife is to align her will and energies with her husband in the tasks of the marriage under God.

It is up to the couple to decide on whether they will follow a traditional or an egalitarian model of marriage. The important matter for a Christian approach to marriage is the love, service, and mutual concern of the partners.

I believe that it is possible for a couple to have a traditional model of marriage structure as their 'philosophy of marriage', while operating as a couple in a very egalitarian way. Another scenario can also occur. A couple may hold to an egalitarian model, while functioning in a very traditional way. We can espouse an ideal, but our actions betray a different approach.

I have suggested that the New Testament's guidance to married couples needs to be understood as application of the Christian message to first-century culture, and that we need to discern the abiding principles that apply to us in a very different culture.

Let us consider how this applies to the way that the wife relates to her husband in the Christian marriage.

We should remember that the Bible does not define marriage roles in detail. For example, it does not say who makes final decisions, or which partner should do what work. Remember the working wives of Bible times, as in Proverbs 31:10-31, where the wife is active in business and work for the family. The focus is on partnership, with nurture and protection calling out loving responsiveness and cooperation.

If the husband's headship no longer contains patriarchal authority, what happens to the wife's calling to submit to her husband?

A different kind of 'submission'

Just as I have suggested that there is a kind of headship ministry for the husband that is not authority to rule over his wife, I want to propose that the Christian wife has a different kind of submission to the traditional pattern.

It does not mean obedience. New Testament scholar B. Ward Powers reminds us that neither in Ephesians 5, nor anywhere else in the New Testament, will there be found an instruction for wives to obey their husbands. 'Obedience is an act; submissiveness is an attitude ... Obedience is not appropriate for a partnership like a marriage; submissiveness is' (Powers, 133).

Whatever pattern of married roles you decide to follow, the Christian wife's position is not inferiority; submission, in Christian terms, does not imply inferiority. It is about service, love and response. Submission is another word for love. 'Submitting to one another does not involve in the least the idea of being substandard; rather it is the calling to serve each other in order to fulfil God's demands' (Olthuis, 144).

The wife's response to her husband will be a thoughtful,

responsible self-offering of heart and life. Our submission to the Lord is our reasonable service (Romans 12:1-2). We are to trust Him and work with Him, and He calls us His friends and co-workers. We are to talk things over with the Lord and seek His will.

The wife's calling in marriage follows the same pattern. It is to be a thoughtful and responsible engagement with her husband in the challenges and tasks of marriage.

The Christian husband and the Christian wife both live together under the authority and protection of their mutual Head, the Lord Jesus Christ. The wife's response to her husband's spiritual leadership is to honour him and cooperate with him in the Lord and for the Lord. She is his helper and partner in the business of marriage and family life.

Here is another parallel between the Christian life and marriage. Just as the believer aligns his or her will with the Lord Jesus, so the Christian wife is to align her will and energies with her husband in the tasks of the marriage under God.

No place for abuse of the other in marriage

Let me be very clear on this: the wife is *not* called to endure abusive treatment at the hands of her husband, and she is not to treat him with disrespect, dishonour, or abuse.

Some husbands and some wives think that the marriage bond gives them the right to behave towards the other in ways that would harm or destroy any other relationship. Why do they think their marriage will survive it?

The Christian faith is clear on this matter: there are *never* any grounds for abusing one's marriage partner, whether it is physical violence, emotional neglect, verbal denigration, financial manipulation, coercive control, or other cruel and unkind acts. We are to live considerately, gently, and kindly with each other (1 Peter 3:7). All unkindness of word and action is ruled out by the call to godly and loving behaviours. 'Love is kind,' says the apostle Paul (1 Corinthians 13:4), and this must happen at home as well as outside.

I have learned in my pastoral ministry that people don't always recognise abuse, either when they receive it or when they are the abusers. Our capacity for self-deception is real.

The husband has no authorisation from God to control, demean, or abuse his wife. It is completely unacceptable for any husband to abuse his wife, and doubly so for any man who wants to follow the Servant Lord who sacrificed and gave His life for His bride, the Church.

Submission and cooperation in marriage does not mean allowing yourself to be abused. Whatever role the Christian wife feels she is called to in marriage, there is no basis for accepting abuse from your husband. Allowing yourself to be abused is not the calling of the Christian wife. The marital partner that is abusive is sinning before God and against the spouse.

I urge the marrying couple to have a difficult but honest conversation in advance about what kind of behaviours should *not* happen in their marriage. Be specific—this could become very important. Your covenant to love each other can include the boundaries of what is unloving behaviour.

When we were engaged, my fiancée told me explicitly that she would not tolerate any physical violence from me: 'Hit me, and I will be out the door.' It was a bit confronting to hear; I had not even considered that possibility. There has never been any abuse in our relationship, I hasten to add. But I am glad she was so clear and in-my-face about it.

It is likely that there will be warning signs of abusive behaviour before the wedding day. These red flags should not be ignored. I have also known a case where the bad behaviour did not show until the deal was sealed and the honeymoon was over, and statistics show that this is unfortunately the way some abusers work.

One of the areas covered in good premarital counselling is

the family background of each party to the prospective marriage, particularly whether there has been abuse in their families of origin. This can be confronting to discuss, but it is worth acknowledging. For some, abuse was part of their family life. Others will be completely naive about this danger and can be unprepared for it. I recall one distressed young wife describing her husband's treatment of her and asking me whether I thought it might be abuse. It certainly was abusive, in my view, and I was very surprised that she did not see it that way.

Some abusive spouses can be very deceptive in the way they charm the partner, up till the day of commitment. The parallel in the Christian life is the darkness and deception of evil in human hearts, against which there is a spiritual gift mentioned by the apostle Paul (the discernment of spirits, 1 Corinthians 12:10—I believe that this is an ability to see what spiritual forces are at work in people and situations). Spiritual warfare is real, and there are dangers abroad.

There is wisdom therefore in the practice of not rushing into commitment, of getting to know the other person in different contexts, in taking the wise counsel of friends, and in prayer for insight. Every marrying partner should be clear on what behaviour is not to be part of their relationship, and this should be part of their mutual commitment.

Service is the way of love

Each partner is to find fulfilment in serving the other—this is the way of Jesus Christ. He set the example of service for His followers:

> 'Whoever wants to be great among you will be your servant, and whoever wants to be first must be the slave of all. For the Son of Man did not come to be

served but to serve and to give his life as a ransom for many.' (Mark 10:44-45, REB)

As you build your marriage, you are working out how to live together and tackle the tasks of your shared life. You must learn the way of love in the daily shared life of your marriage.

In the next section, we will look at how you furnish or decorate this house of your marriage—how you fill your relationship with love. You make a vow to love, and it will take a lifetime to fulfil it.

Let's dig deeply into the marvellous mystery of love: how the two become one.

Reflection/Discussion: The wife and her husband

1. Discuss how the husband and the wife can share a spiritual partnership under the Headship of the Lord Jesus Christ.
2. Talk about what kinds of behaviours are properly described as 'abusive'. How do you *not* want to be treated? Make a promise to each other *never* to treat each other this way.

PART 4
DECORATION—FILLING YOUR MARRIAGE WITH LOVE

Your marriage house must be filled with the furnishings of love, as you make a home of warmth and affection through growing oneness.

17 GROWING TOGETHER IN MARRIAGE

Becoming one, growing into a deeper unity, is the calling of marriage.

The wedding vows, observes Mike Mason, only take about thirty seconds to say, but keeping them is the work of a lifetime (Mason, 93).

The rituals, ceremonies, and splendid clothing that mark most weddings celebrate the importance of the occasion. With only a few variations, the couple are dressed in beautiful clothes for their roles, and there are similar rituals in most weddings, even across cultures. They are beautiful on their wedding day, but the real beauty of their marriage is their growing oneness in love.

The marriage service reminds us that marriage is a calling to grow into a deepening personal union of love and life:

'It is a lifelong union in which a man and a woman are called so to give themselves in body, mind, and spirit, and so to respond, that from their union will grow a deepening knowledge and love of each other.' (Marriage AAPB Second Form, 560)

In this section we will consider how the couple go about building on the design plan of marriage—how they will build their relationship, to paint, decorate and furnish (as it were) the house of their love.

Lifelong growth into oneness

The marriage service makes a declaration that the man and the woman are now 'one', yet it also marks their calling to grow into a deeper oneness. The two *become* one on their wedding day; they continue *becoming* one, day by day.

However, there is a unique and individual element in every marriage service: the 'persons' who exchange the vows: *this particular* man, *this particular* woman. Marriage is the uniting of *this man N* and *this woman N*. It is two unique individuals who marry.

A healthy marital relationship will mean that the two people grow in their understanding of each other. They gain a deeper knowledge of the other's 'personhood' and find ways to show love to this other, unique person.

In recent years we have learned about how people have their own preferred 'love-languages'—ways of receiving and giving love (Chapman, 1995). The husband and the wife will need to keep working at the task of understanding and loving the real other person with whom they are united in covenant. The strengths and weaknesses of each other's personalities will be factors in the union.

The early stage of a relationship between a man and a woman is usually marked by the excitement of romantic love, which is largely our expectations and idealistic hopes for personal fulfilment. Studies have shown that it takes about four years of marriage (on average) for the misty, romantic idealisations to clear, and then the couple can get down to the task of loving each other as real people, not as bearers of each other's fantasies and hopes (see Very Well Mind, *The Four Stages of Relationships*).

Knowing Christ and knowing Him better

In this calling to grow together, we find another resonance between being married and being a Christian. In the relationship-union of the Christian and the Lord, there is also a process of growing together.

When we come to faith in Christ, we come to know Him as our Lord, but we then begin to know Him better as we draw closer to Him and experience His friendship. The apostle Paul describes this paradox of knowing Christ and wanting to know Him better:

> 'I want to know Christ—yes, to know the power of his resurrection and participation in his sufferings, becoming like him in his death, and so, somehow, attaining to the resurrection from the dead.' (Philippians 3:10-11, NIV)

The parallels in these two relationships (marital and faith) are instructive.

The married couple become one in the wedding, and then spend a lifetime becoming more united and knowing each other better. The Christian becomes one with Christ, and then begins the lifetime—an eternity—of knowing God better.

For followers of Christ, the growth of the marriage love-relationship reminds us that in our relationship with God, He invites us to a deepening, growing relationship with us in Jesus Christ. He wants to reveal His real Self to us, and for us to share our real selves with Him in a genuine relationship.

The early days of your Christian commitment are often exciting, but usually give way to periods of harder spiritual growth and personal change. There can be an idealistic early love for the Lord that is similar to the excitement and idealism of initial romantic love.

We start with the 'our Father in heaven' stage as the focus of our journey; then in time we must face the 'deliver us from evil' stage of spiritual struggle and challenge. This is what 1 John 2:12-14 describes: there are stages of spiritual growth and challenge.

We cannot stay infants in our spiritual lives forever; we need to grow in wisdom and obedience as we face challenges.

The Christian's experience of church relationships has its idealistic stage too, which must give way to the reality of living as a fallen person among other fallible ones. Dietrich Bonhoeffer pointed out this dispelling of illusions about church relationships: 'When the morning mists of dreams vanish, then dawns the bright day of Christian fellowship' (Bonhoeffer, 1954, 17).

Growing in closeness in your marriage

Your marriage will likely follow the same pattern.

The misty-morning dreams of romance are wonderful, but they must pass when we get down to living together as real, fallible people. The enthusiasm of early love must be tested by difficulties and reality.

If you are a sincere follower of Jesus Christ who gets married, you will not be surprised then to find out that your marriage relationship will take time to grow through the mutual limitations, foolishness, immaturities, and sometimes real sins against each other.

In your spiritual life with the Lord, you probably know already that personal growth in self-awareness and holiness takes time, and requires humility, confession, and sometimes a deal of painful struggle. Holiness takes time to develop; so, also, does being a mature, loving spouse.

Draw closer to the Lord, draw closer to one another

If you both share a personal faith in God, then as you each draw closer to God, you should find that you are drawing closer to each other in Christ. I use a diagram to illustrate this process. Think of a triangle, with the man and the woman at the base corners, and God at the apex corner. As you each draw closer to God, you will, on the 'triangle' of your shared relationship with God, become closer to one another.

Give thought then about how you will draw closer to the Lord and get to know Him better as the years go by (2 Peter 3:18). We will return in the final chapter to the issue of how to be Christians in your marriage together.

Think of how you and your marriage partner can develop a deeper knowledge and love of each other. What will you do to foster this? Watch, lest you start to drift apart.

My wife and I took a weekend away after our silver wedding anniversary, to spend time talking about our relationship. We did the *Enrich* marital inventory, a questionnaire we each completed about how our marriage was going, and took the results with us for discussion. It was a beautiful and encouraging time together, as we reflected on the marriage union we had been building and talked about where we wanted to develop.

In marriage, as in the spiritual life, we are called to press on towards the goal of a closer relationship (Philippians 3:14). This principle of 'always going forward' applies to both the Christian life, and the married life:

> 'We begin to go backward as soon as we cease to go forward. There is no holding our own in the spiritual life, except by continually holding more.' (Jowett, 135)

Reflection/Discussion: Growing together in marriage

1. How well do you understand each other? Have you been together long enough to see the real person whom you will marry? Have you talked over the many issues about which you will need agreement or mutual understanding? Doing a premarital inventory such as *Prepare/Enrich* (prepare-enrich.com) about your mutual expectations is a good preparation.
2. How will you develop your relationship *after* you are married?

18 THE TWO BECOME ONE—BY ABANDONING SELFISHNESS

The union of one flesh does not remove the selfhood of each partner; it means the abandoning of independent self-centredness.

Marriage is a school for learning unselfishness, and the course of lessons is never finished. To build a union out of two persons, the couple must learn to deal with self-centredness.

The wedding vows in the Anglican tradition derive from the medieval English marriage service, and they reflect the biblical, Christian understanding of marriage.

> 'I, N, in the presence of God, take you N to be my wife/husband, to have and to hold from this day forward, for better, for worse, for richer, for poorer, in sickness and in health, to love and to cherish, as long as we both shall live. This is my solemn vow and promise.' (Marriage APBA Second Form, 563)

With these words, the couple commits to obey God's

calling of them to oneness, as Jesus said: 'and the two will become one flesh' (Mark 10:8, NIV).

The two become one flesh

What does it mean, the two becoming one? We will explore this union of the two in the next few chapters.

The two become *one flesh*, says the Bible (Genesis 2:24). The basic idea is that the man and the woman join in a union that can do something together, as one unit, which neither of them can do on their own: produce children, offspring. Their union has a literal, physical (fleshly) basis. It is the biological action of reproduction that the two complementary humans do together.

But the two becoming one goes beyond this procreative level. It requires them to join their *lives* together, not just their *bodies* (sexually). God's plan, and the wisdom of nature, is that the children that are *pro-created*, will be nurtured in a loving union, the family.

This joining is a covenant commitment. The wedding vows are promises to *cleave* to one another in the sense of Genesis 2:24, to use an older translation. Another translation is to *join*. The word denotes two things that stick together very firmly. It is a Bible word, a covenant word. The Lord God calls us to cleave or stick to Him, as He promises to stick to His people (Deuteronomy 10:20). The couple are to stick together in a promised covenant or commitment.

Your self does not disappear

How do the two people unite? Do they lose their individuality, with either one submerged in the other, or both merging and becoming fused? We know that there can be serious differences that bring conflict between the two. Here is the tension—the challenge of working on separateness and closeness, on autonomy and intimacy.

There is a difference between selfhood and selfishness. There is nothing wrong with being a 'self', a person, with your individual personality, values, and rights. It is not selfish to want to be a person with choices and boundaries respected by others.

The oneness that Jesus refers to is a union that does not destroy the *selfhood* of each partner but comes from the abandonment of independent *self-centredness*. We choose to include another self in our own world, to join our own self to the other person's self.

They are no longer two separate parties engaging in a power struggle or even a contract with each other. Mike Mason puts it well: 'A marriage is not a joining of two worlds, but an abandoning of two worlds in order that one new one might be formed' (Mason, 91).

The 'me' and the 'we' join

Picture your marriage relationship as two partially overlapping circles. The husband and the wife share much together, and their common love and life together now form part of their individual lives (their own circles). The joining of their lives forms out of the two circles, a new united entity (overlapping circles). 'So, they are no longer two but one flesh,' said Jesus. They are one 'unit' made up of two persons.

Thus, the two people 'become one' by joining their *selves* together and leaving independence behind. They no longer think of themselves as separate selves but as a 'we', a union.

They make this unity work by countering their self-centredness. They try to always consider the other's interests and needs as well as their own issues. The apostle Paul defined the essence of love as not seeking our own good but the good of others (1 Corinthians 10:24), and this is central to married love. From now on there will be a 'we' that cannot be separated from the 'me' of each partner. They promise to have and to hold—the promise to cleave, or cling to one another, in loving commitment whatever happens. The 'we' becomes as important as the 'me'.

The Christian parallels: two becoming one

This important challenge of how the two can become one in their marriage can be illuminated by the Christian faith, which is about another relationship in which the two are called to become one in purpose and love.

There are two areas of the Christian life in which we get an experience of how the two become one: our fellowship with others, as we are called to love them; and our union with the Lord Jesus Christ.

Love for others puts them into our lives. The call to make the 'we' important to the 'me' is a basic Christian calling. We are to consider the good or well-being of others as much as or more than we cater for our own wants. The apostle Paul puts Christ forward as the supreme example of self-giving for others in Philippians 2:5-11, and draws the application for our relationships:

> 'Don't do anything for selfish purposes, but with humility think of others as better than yourselves. Instead of each person watching out for their own good, watch out for what is better for others.' (Philippians 2:3-4, CEB)

The Christian faith does not only teach about unselfishness, it also gives us a profound model of how two selves can become one in a self-giving union. The Christian life is also an illustration of two becoming one in the union of the believer and the Lord.

Union with Christ

God has committed His own Self to us in Christ (Romans 8:31-34) and we give ourselves to Him in return (Romans 12:1-2). We enter a covenant commitment with each other: the Lord, and the Christian disciple.

The follower of Christ is united to Christ in a close, spiritual relationship. We are joined to God through Christ, as branches to the vine (John 15:1-8); we have died and risen with Christ; we are members of the Body of Christ, the Church. We cannot and must not act as if we are 'not in Christ'.

The believer unites with the Lord in a mutual love-commitment that involves an interdependent relationship of giving themselves to each other. The Lord God is in our lives and our lives are 'in Christ'.

The apostle Paul expresses this well:

'I have been crucified with Christ and I no longer live, but Christ lives in me. And the life that I now live in my body, I live by faith, indeed, by the faithfulness of God's Son, who loved me and gave himself for me.' (Galatians 2:20, CEB)

For the Christian, there is no longer 'my life' apart from 'Christ in me, and with me'. There is a real spiritual 'we' now.

This mysterious mutual indwelling is the heart of the Christian life. God 'lives' in us in the person of the Holy Spirit, who bears witness in our hearts that we are the children of God (Romans 8:14-16). God is close to us—closer to us than we ourselves—and we are now inextricably connected to

God. The life we live, says the apostle Paul, is lived *in Christ*, in union with Him.

The 'we' dimension of love

This means the Christian, although a servant and child of God, lives in a 'we' dimension: God and me, together. This is the mystery of love: we live in the life of the other, and the other is part of us.

When people encounter us, in a sense they are meeting someone in whom God is present. Jesus prayed like this to God His Father (John 17), that He would be in His disciples, and they would be in Him and the Father.

This union of the Lord and the believer does not obliterate our selfhood, so that we cease to be real partners with God. The Lord who lives in us and with us does not take over us so that we lose our integrity and responsibility. That over-control of our selfhood is not God's loving way, and neither should a husband or wife think that they should squelch the personhood of their spouse.

The married couple will unite in love so much that they will live in each other's hearts and lives. The 'we' will be strong and real alongside the 'me'.

This 'we' dimension of love has been expressed succinctly by Robert Law, a commentator on First John:

> 'One finds one's richest satisfaction in the happiness of others, one's own fullest self-realization in promoting theirs. Love seeks not its own yet makes all things its own. It is the utmost enrichment and enlargement of Life. "My beloved is mine"—a possession of which nothing can rob me. The more perfect the love, the more completely achieved is this mysterious result, this self-enlargement by self-communication, this self-losing, which is the real self-finding. If I love my

neighbour as myself, I regale myself with his prosperity, even as I share the bitter cup of his adversity; I am honoured in his praise, promoted in his advancement, gladdened in his joy, even as I am humbled in his shame or distressed in his sin.' (Law, 78)

This Love, supremely revealed in the love of God, is the love we seek in marriage.

We see this in the grief that lovers feel when they lose their beloved to death. They feel that they have lost part of themselves, which is true psychologically. The 'we' has been sundered.

This is why there is a striking resonance between the wedding vows of the couple to each other, and the baptismal vows of the new disciple of Christ. In both covenants the parties make strong commitments to one another and give themselves to one another. The disciple gives up independence of God and renounces selfishness; so do the married couple in their vows and commitment to each other.

Just as the Christian lives 'in Christ' and Christ lives in us by the Spirit, so the married couple grow to live *in* each other, in a mutual indwelling that is something like the union those in Christ have with the Lord.

We can always gain a closer walk with Jesus, and the married couple is invited to draw closer to one another in their union of lives.

The Christian life is about surrendering a 'me' circle of life, for a 'we' life with the Lord God. The married couple likewise each surrenders their 'me' independence to share a new life together, as 'we'.

Reflection/Discussion: The two become one—by abandoning selfishness

1. In your present stage of your relationship, what is the balance of the 'me' and the 'we'? Do you feel that your own selfhood is being absorbed by your partner?
2. How is the relationship of the Lord God and the believer a model for the interdependent unity God calls married partners to fulfil?

19 THE TWO BECOME ONE—BY JOINING TWO WHOLE PEOPLE

> Marriage calls each party to give their whole selves to each other, and in doing so, they do not lose themselves but find a new and larger self in each other.

The pledge of marriage that accompanies the giving of the rings in the marriage service conveys the commitment of the whole person:

> 'N, with this ring I wed you; with all that I am and all that I have, I honour you; in the name of God. Amen. ... N, may God enable us to grow in love together.' (Marriage AAPB Second Form, 564)

The vows of the marriage service call for the joining of two lives into a new unity—a unity made up of two different people. They give themselves to each other.

Let's continue to explore the mystery of how the two can become one in marriage.

Marriage calls each party to give their whole selves to each other. Does this mean that each person gives up being a full self, a whole, complete person? If the two become one, does this mean that they each must give away half of themselves? Must they each sacrifice their individual self to the new partnership?

Losing your self?

Sadly, this is the case in some marriages. Partners can feel that they are being dominated, or absorbed, or controlled by the other. One partner must give way all the time, or have their personal values denied or avoided for the sake of the marriage. They must deny or hide their true self, to make the relationship work.

Counsellors call this 'de-selfing': when too much of the genuine self becomes negotiable or suppressed to avoid a conflict with the partner. To create a workable marriage means that one or other must become a diminished person, half a person (Stevens, 105).

While there must be a giving up of self-centredness and selfishness, this is not the same as 'de-selfing', which is a denial of one's proper 'self'.

In marriage, the selfhood of a partner can be suppressed unhealthily. The marriage can be working (temporarily or inadequately) because one person is inappropriately compensating for the other. The problems of the partner are causing a loss of a whole-person union. This can even become a deliberate coercive control of one spouse by the other, a form of abuse.

Each person in marriage has a proper 'self' that needs to be respected and allowed to exist. When one dominates or controls the other unreasonably, squashing the personality of the partner, there is a denial of his/her proper individuality and selfhood. Giving up selfishness does not mean giving up self—your personal selfhood.

Selfhood is not selfishness

Christians can make a mistake in this matter. *Selfishness* is not the same as proper regard for our *selfhood*. Some Christians have confused the call to reject selfishness, and to renounce the sinful nature that we still have in us (Mark 8:34-35; 1 Corinthians 13:4) with a call to reject our *selves*. We can confuse hating ourselves (self-rejection), with opposition to pride, self-love, self-sufficiency.

Many people allow themselves to undervalue their *self*, out of a low view of themselves, thinking that this is selflessness. It is not God's will to hate and reject yourself as a person, thinking it is godly unselfishness. Hatred of our self is contrary to God's value of our selves. There is a proper self-regard that is not selfishness.

If a marriage is to work well, it needs to be a relationship in which each person can find fulfilment as a person. It is not selfish to want to find self-fulfilment.

When a marriage partner is squashed or dominated by the spouse, then they cannot flourish. Selfishness is the problem, not self-fulfilment. Both partners need to bring their complete selves to the marriage. 'You have to have two wheels for a bicycle, and you need two complete persons for a marriage to work' (Greteman, 54).

We can think of this in terms of the diagram of two circles, joined and overlapping. What if one person's 'circle' (wishes, choices, views, etc.) completely covers the other person's 'circle'? The two have not become one; one has taken over the other.

There are differences that will need to be resolved, accepted, or accommodated. For two people to grow in a union of heart and lives they will both need to accommodate and serve each other, denying their selfishness for the sake of the union. Yes, there must be give and take.

The marriage vows express our commitment to give our

real selves to each other for the sake of the development of the potential of each other. Surely this is what the word 'cherish' means—to prize and nourish the other person, to bring out the best in our spouse. Marriage grows stronger by nourishing and fulfilling the individuals who love each other.

Giving ourselves, gaining a new self

Once again, we can find help from the pattern of the Christian's relationship with God. Behind the Christian marriage vows stands the Divine-human love bond between Christ and His people.

God gives His real Self to us in Jesus Christ. As the apostle Paul eloquently stated: 'He didn't spare his own Son but gave him up for us all. Won't he also freely give us all things with him?' (Romans 8:32, CEB).

In effect, God has given us a promise that could be stated in the words from the marriage service: 'with all that I am, and all that I have, I honour you' (Marriage AAPB Second Form, 564).

By giving His very self to us in the person of His Son Jesus Christ, the living God has given us His all, the greatest honour we could receive. 'See what kind of love the Father has given to us in that we should be called God's children, and that is what we are!' (1 John 3:1, CEB).

The Christian in turn gives his/her whole, real self to the Lord, presenting our bodies 'as a living sacrifice that is holy and pleasing to God' (Romans 12:1, CEB), in effect repeating back to Him the same words of the wedding service: 'with all that I am, and all that I have, I honour you.' The words of the vow from the 1662 Anglican matrimony service convey the idea even more forcefully: 'with my body I thee worship.' As we give our whole self to God, body and soul, as our proper worship, so we give our whole self, our real self, to our spouse in the marriage pledge.

This is the aim of our Lord's commitment to His bride, the Church.

> '... just like Christ loved the church and gave himself for her. He did this to make her holy by washing her in a bath of water with the word. He did this to present himself with a splendid church, one without any sort of stain or wrinkle on her clothes, but rather one that is holy and blameless.' (Ephesians 5:25-27, CEB)

In marriage, each partner aims to serve the other, to bring the other to his or her fullest potential as a person. Hopefully, the loving union helps remove some of the spots and wrinkles.

The service—the self-giving—that sets us free

The fulfilment that comes from giving our lives to God and His giving Himself to us is well expressed in the statement from the Anglican morning prayer service: 'whose service is perfect freedom' (Morning Prayer AAPB First Form, 28). When we serve the Lord, we do not find ourselves demeaned or oppressed: we find ourselves fulfilled and set free.

Marriage will reflect the way of Divine love when each partner finds personal fulfilment in the sharing of their love.

By giving our self to each other, we gain an expanded self, filled with love.

Reflection/Discussion: The two become one—by joining two whole people

1. How will you try to make your marriage a growing experience of personal wholeness for each partner?

2. Your marriage vows are your commitment to bring out the best in each other. How are you currently helping each other develop in maturity and wholeness? How will you pursue this intentionally in your marriage?

20 THE TWO BECOME ONE—BY UNCONDITIONAL LOVE

The love that is declared and witnessed in a marriage service is a statement of faith, hope and love.

A Christian wedding is a startling combination of hope-filled celebration of the couple's love and very realistic —even shocking—vows, that envisage the possibilities of difficulties and hardships.

The Christian marriage service stands out for this realistic emphasis on how love is expressed in the will to persevere in being loving, whatever happens. Truly, the apostle Paul was right to praise love for its ability to always trust, always hope, always endure (1 Corinthians 13:7).

The vows explicitly rule out any unspoken qualifications to the promises, such as, 'as long as I find it fulfilling, or not a burden to me, or as long as we are still in love', and so on.

The husband and wife promise in the marriage vows that they will stick at the task of loving, protecting, and cherishing each other whatever happens in their life together, as the well-known words convey:

'... for better for worse, for richer, for poorer, in sickness and in health, to love and to cherish, as long as we both shall live.' (Marriage AAPB Second Form, 562)

The words 'for better, for worse' are comprehensive. The love proclaimed in these marriage vows is described in terms of unconditional commitment to help and serve, through thick and thin.

On several occasions in my pastoral ministry, I have reminded a married person or a couple that they had vowed to stay together through the situation they now find themselves in—namely, the 'worse'.

The commitment line holds steady

I use an illustration to explain two components of the marriage relationship. Think of two lines running from the wedding ceremony. The first is the *relationship* line, which rises or falls depending on how their relationship is going and is affected by internal and external stresses (sickness, financial troubles, failures towards each other, etc).

The second line running from their wedding is the *commitment* line. This is their solid promise to stick with the marriage and stay committed whatever the challenges. This line should not rise or fall with their relationship; it should stay fixed and strong. It will give them motivation to stay together and draw together, to work on their relationship when things sag, or they hit problems.

Their marriage must not ride only on their relationship but on their commitment.

> 'Marriages which are dependent on love fall apart, or at best are in for a stormy time of it. But marriages which consistently look back to their vows, to those wild promises made before God, and which trust Him

to make sense out of them, find a continual source of strength and renewal.' (Mason, 95)

Right at the beginning of their formal union, the husband and wife count the cost of commitment to each other. They recognise that to love one another will be a challenge sometimes when life gets difficult and problems mount.

Sometimes in marriages, it will only be the solid commitment to hold on that keeps the union together, until, hopefully, the relationship line rises. Holding the commitment firm may be the key to dealing with relational problems. It will be their married commitment that supports their love.

'For worse'

The possibility of the marriage reaching a 'worse' stage must be admitted. While no one wants to mention or think of it at a marriage service, we all know that the biggest challenge to their love will be their own sinfulness, either in its active form of deliberate unfaithfulness or abuse, or in the weakness of fallible human nature. We are sinners, and sin often means 'falling short' of who we should be. This is recognised in the prayers, when the minister asks God to 'strengthen their wills to keep the promises they have made' (Marriage AAPB Second Form, 566).

The Christian going into marriage will already be aware of how weak and fallible he/she is, due to the remaining reality of sin and human limitations. If we pray for daily forgiveness of our sins, we should not be surprised that 'sin' will be a persistent challenge in our marriage.

The Christian life has its 'worse'

Christians know that we will have to deal with the ongoing challenges of our fallen natures, our limitations. Our obedience to God will require commitment and effort. Church life and our own failures will make it hard and disappointing at times.

Our marriage will demand a similar strenuous effort to deal with our limitations and failures. The words of the vow virtually admit this fact: 'This is my solemn vow and promise' (Marriage AAPB Second Form, 563). The love that is on view is their love *in the future*. The vow is an act of faith about what the couple will do together with their present relationship.

The love that is declared and witnessed in a marriage service is a statement of faith, hope, and love. Just as the Christian sets out on the way of the cross, knowing the rewards and the cost of loving the Lord Jesus Christ, so also the married couple set out on their life-journey together, counting the cost and challenges that may lie ahead.

Life can be a battlefield, spiritually

The wedding vows recognise that life is a battlefield, a struggle against forces outside and inside, that will attack the love and commitment of the couple.

Here is another resonance with the Christian faith. Followers of Jesus Christ understand that life itself is a spiritual battleground against all sorts of forces and influences that work against faith in God and ongoing obedience. They will know that there are spiritual, anti-God forces working in society and within our hearts to damage us, and our marriages will be targets of this struggle (Ephesians 6:10-20).

They will not be surprised that their marriages will be caught up in this spiritual warfare. The couple should not forget the bigger spiritual battle that is affecting their relationship. Dan Allender and Tremper Longman draw attention to this:

'Married people confront life as a battle. As intimate allies, they push back the chaos. With the power of God, marriage is an awesome calling and at times a delightful prelude of heaven. But no matter what joy or what sense of meaning is found in marriage, it is always involved in a war. At times marriage itself is part of the war.' (Allender & Longman, 346)

The Christian couple should remember that, in their marriage, they are still on the field of the spiritual battle. Prayer and all the resources of God are there for the couple's help. This is why we pray that God may 'strengthen their wills to keep the promises they have made'.

Reflection/Discussion: The two become one—by unconditional love

1. Think of your love for each other as made up of emotions, needs, attraction, hopes, and volitions (the will). How important is the commitment of your *will*, to keep the promises?
2. The Christian life is part of a spiritual battle (Ephesians 6:10-20). How might the spiritual war affect your marriage in Christ?

21 MARRIAGE AND THE TWO KINDS OF LOVE

God is the source of Love, both natural and supernatural, and you can draw on God's love to empower your married love.

Wedding services are celebrations of love, and we know how our society dwells on the romance of love.

One of the most popular readings for a Christian marriage service is the famous exhortation to love by the apostle Paul, found in 1 Corinthians 13 (1 Corinthians 12:31–13:13). It is a beautiful description of love—the love needed for good relationships to flourish and grow.

Read it carefully, however, and you will realise that it is not describing *romantic* love. It is about how loving others will call for us to be patient; how we must not be rude, or jealous, or arrogant. Love means we must not be rude or easily angered. This kind of love is grounded, realistic.

The apostle Paul lists fifteen qualities of love in action, and right in the centre of the list is the attribute that I believe is the core, the essence of love: love does not 'seek its own advantage' (1 Corinthians 13:5, CEB). Literally, it reads: 'does not seek its own'. This idea is expanded a few chapters earlier as seeking the good of the other, not self (1 Corinthians 10:24). Love is 'other-person-centred'.

This passage on Love does apply to marriages, because this kind of love—the enduring, unselfish, hopeful love—is precisely the sort of divinely inspired love that we need.

Yes, 'love' features a lot in the marriage service, but it is not just romantic love that is on view. There are two loves celebrated in the Christian wedding service, and both are needed for a loving marriage.

Natural love and supernatural love, gifts from God

There is another kind of love, apart from the romantic kind, that is the focus of a Christian wedding service; it will be essential to a successful marriage.

Marriage requires a combination of *natural* love and *supernatural* love. I believe that this is a distinctively Christian insight into marriage-love.

Marriage is based on the natural love of the woman and the man. The wedding service states this in its words and in the Bible passages used. God the Creator has made us as His creatures, male and female, and endowed us with desires and capacities for physical and emotional love. There is nothing wrong with this love of attraction and desire; it is God-designed.

This natural love is made up of sexual attraction, personal liking, common interests and values, and other factors that draw them together, a mysterious chemistry that is beyond the analysis of the couple themselves. Compatibility and chemistry are important parts of this natural love-bond.

A successful marriage builds on this initial chemistry and compatibility, adding to natural attraction the tested experiences of friendship and affection born of the shared tasks of marriage and family life. Communication and good conflict-resolution skills will be needed to keep the quality of the natural love strong.

Liking and *loving* are two ways of distinguishing these loves. Liking is a natural, almost instinctive thing, made up of compatibility, attraction, chemistry. Loving is a deliberate choice of the will to be loving and kind to the other person.

We can call these two kinds of love 'affectionate love' and 'commitment love'. It is not that the latter is devoid of emotion; God's love for us is full of tenderness. But it comes from God's own loving nature; it flows out to others.

The attraction, the chemistry, of your initial liking for the other person may wane or be challenged by how they behave. The nature of married love will usually change from the initial romance, through friendship, and be tested by commitment and life together.

You don't have to be a follower of Jesus Christ to have this giving-love. Human love in marriage, family, and friendships often rises to this beautiful self-giving love. I believe that all couples who stay together and grow in love, whether followers of Christ or not, will know something of giving-love in their relationship.

God's kind of love

The Christian gospel reminds us of another kind of love, which the Christian husband and wife already know about, the Divine kind of love (in Greek: *agape*, pronounced 'agapee').

This is the love that God has shown us in Christ: kindness and generosity to people, despite our rejection and failure. It is a love that proceeds from the Divine Lover and is not dependent on the qualities of the beloved.

In marriage, as in life generally, we need to have God's heart in our heart, so that we can keep loving the person who we do not always find attractive, when our natural liking fails.

God is the source of love found in us. We are vessels that can show the love that God has put in us by nature and by His supernatural gift. He is the fountain; we are not the source, simply the cups that hold the love He has given us.

God in Christ has shown us the *pattern of love*, this extravagant generosity, and He has also made available to us His *power for love* by the Holy Spirit (see Ephesians 3:14-21).

This is the kind of love that is most clearly shown by God towards us, in Jesus Christ. Christians know that this love can fill us and infuse itself into our natural kinds of love. Remember that in Christ you have a connection with God, the fountain of love (1 John 4:7-21). We have a constantly renewing supply of love on which to draw.

The marriage service prays for this kind of love in your lives together:

> 'God our Father ... so bless these two persons as they pledge their lives to each other, that their love may evermore grow to be the true reflection of your love for us all: through Jesus Christ our Lord.' (Marriage AAPB Second Form, 562)

In a Christian wedding service, you are not just saying, 'Look at us, how much we love one another!' You are also saying, 'Help us love one another, Lord, by pouring into us your kind of love, when our natural love is not strong.'

Whether you have the 1 Corinthians 13 Bible reading in your service or not, read it together and make a checklist of the qualities of love in action. This list can remind you about how your love for each other should be put into practice.

Reflection/Discussion: Marriage and the two kinds of love

1. How prepared are you to seek a *supernatural* kind of love in your marriage? Put into your own words the difference between affectionate love and commitment love.
2. Love seeks for the good of the other person. Do you know this type of love—this kindness and giving-love that is not quenched by rejection or unattractiveness?

22 THE TWO BECOME ONE—BY FULFILLING EACH OTHER

The calling of marriage is to help one's beloved to become the best person they can be, with a beauty of character that is inspired by love.

The bride and the groom prepare to make themselves beautiful and presentable on their wedding day. They have never looked better, and probably will never match this again!

They do it for each other. The bride presents herself adorned for her husband and the husband wants to look his best for his bride.

Far beyond their external appearance, the real task after the wedding is to help each other grow in the inner beauty of character and personal maturity.

Their marriage commitment is a dedication to be the best person for the other, and to bring the best out of the other—to develop, cherish and fulfil each other. They promise to find their personal happiness in the welfare of the other.

From now on, they are interdependent, defined in relation to each other. The husband's personhood is now defined in relation to his wife and the wife's personhood is now inseparable from her relationship to her husband. How is she developing as a person, in this calling to be a wife? How can the husband be fulfilled and happy in his calling to be a husband, if his wife is not doing well in their relationship? (A truth expressed in the wry proverb: 'happy wife, happy life.')

Individual fulfilment through helping the other to fulfilment has been explained well by Iain McGilchrist:

> 'A good relationship is one in which each party is maximally fulfilled as a differentiated individual, without this in any way detracting from the relationship, but rather being a condition of the possibility of a good relationship at all—and as a consequence of such a relationship.' (McGilchrist, Vol. I, 394)

The spouses must remember that, from now on, it will not be possible to find individual fulfilment in their marriage if their actions abuse, neglect, hurt, or squash the other person.

Find your fulfilment in the flourishing of your partner

The secret of marriage is the law of love: to find one's own fulfilment in the fulfilment of the other person. It is a calling to serve your partner's well-being and their flourishing. The husband and the wife will make a great marriage by working to nurture and help each other grow as people.

In the Christian life, we know that Christ cares for us as His body, one with Himself. The Christian also knows that harming another Christian is hurting the Body of Christ, the Church, as the apostle Paul observes: 'If one part suffers, all the parts suffer with it ...' (1 Corinthians 12:26, CEB).

Likewise, when a husband abuses his wife, or a wife abuses her husband—there are many ways of abusing—who do they think they are hurting? They not only hurt the other, but they also harm themselves by damaging the relationship. This is the reality of interdependence as married persons.

The apostle Paul makes the same point for husbands who are united with their wives:

> 'That's how husbands ought to love their wives—in the same way as they do their own bodies. Anyone who loves his wife loves himself. No one ever hates his own body, but feeds it and takes care of it just like Christ does for the church because we are parts of his body.' (Ephesians 5:28-30, CEB)

Love that fulfils us

The Christian gospel points us to the truth that God in Christ has dedicated Himself to making us, the Church, His bride, beautiful, perfected, transformed by loving, sacrificial service. Recall the apostle Paul's words about how Christ loves the Church, His bride, and gives Himself for us to perfect us (Ephesians 5:25-27).

Your marriage starts with the wedding service displaying the *external* beautification of garments and grooming, by which you seek to present your most attractive self to each other. Your marriage task moving forward is to help each other grow in *inner* beautification of character through love and service—to serve our spouse in love, to help her or him to become the best person, with a beauty inspired by love.

We sometimes see the mature product of married beautification in the mutual love of an old married couple at the end of their life together. On your wedding day, try to imagine how beautiful and attractive in character your partner will look at the end of your marriage!

Love is still challenged, however, by our human desires and preferences. How can two people grow in oneness, when they have a conflict of their wills about some issues?

Reflection/Discussion: The two become one—by fulfilling each other

1. Think about how God works to fulfil us, to bring out the best in us. Are there clues here for married partners to follow in order to fulfil each other?
2. What future would make each of you feel fulfilled —your personal dreams? Share your aspirations and exchange a promise to work to fulfil and respect each other's dreams.

23 THE TWO BECOME ONE—BY MUTUAL SUBMISSION OF WILLS

Mutual submission is an attitude of cooperative service towards others, for their benefit. It is the very opposite to asserting your own rights.

There are no declarations of 'the husband's rights' and 'the wife's rights' in the Christian marriage service.

There is no section of the wedding service or in the marriage licence in which each party can list their conditions and what they want to get out of the relationship. It is not like a contract where the rights of each party are stipulated.

Every married couple will find that they have a contest of wills about some issue. It may be a minor matter or a major principle. What then will the couple do? My wife and I have been married for forty-seven years, so we have had some experience with the clash of wills!

We have talked these disagreements over—sometimes at length—until we reach a decision that we both own. Speaking personally, time has shown me that my first position often was not as good as my wife's; she was right, and I was wrong. Often, we give way to the other, realising that the matter is not that significant or that our unity and love is more important.

The most significant factor in resolving our contest of wills, however, is the resolve we each made to be accommodating and cooperative with each other. We decided that we cannot prevail over each other, as if we were independent individuals with rights to assert.

A declaration of non-independence

Marriage vows are a surrender of each person's right to act as an independent person. From this day on, the couple choose to yield their individual wills to a mutual submission or yielding of wills in the new interdependent bond of a married couple. This is what 'living together according to God's law' means—to unite wills together in a mutual submission to one another (Ephesians 5:17-33).

The wedding service is built around vows (promises) and obligations, not conditions or rights. The emphasis is on what the bride and the groom each promise to do, and what their responsibilities are to each other and, in the Christian wedding, these promises are made before God.

The surprising grace of submission

There is a general Christian principle about yielding our wills to each other. It is called 'submission'. To submit to others is to be prepared to fit in with and respect others. We are ready to put the needs and rights of others before our own agendas.

Mutual submission is an attitude of cooperative service towards others, for their benefit. It is the very opposite to asserting your own rights.

'Submission' is a word that sounds harsh in the ears of modern Western people, but Christians know better. We have learned the beauty of submission from seeing it in our Lord Jesus Christ, who surrendered His rights to serve us with a sacrificial love, not squashing His own will but dedicating it to do the will of the Father (Philippians 2:1-11; John 6:38).

We have learned about submission too in our own relationship with God, as we pray for God's will—not our own—to be done on earth (as Jesus taught us in the Lord's Prayer, Matthew 6:10), and that following Christ means surrendering our independent wills, to choose and to work God's will (Philippians 2:13).

United to the Lord by faith and through His Spirit, we no longer seek to act as independent, self-governing people. United to our spouse in the bond of marriage, we no longer seek to act as independent persons with competing wills. Our submission to others is out of respect for Christ (Ephesians 5:21).

Two wills can work in harmony

In the Christian vision of marriage, each party will work with the other to build their union of heart, mind, and wills. This harmony of wills is probably the biggest challenge of marriage, as Mike Mason notes:

> 'Even the closest of couples will inevitably find themselves engaged in a struggle of wills, for marriage is a wild, audacious attempt at an almost impossible degree of cooperation between two powerful centres of self-assertion ... No marriage can succeed unless it is permeated, saturated, with this spirit of acquiescence, of continual giving in, of gracious and willing compliance.' (Mason, 139, 145)

Does this sound dangerous? The commitment to yield one's will to the other is not a decision to be a doormat, to be abused or crushed. The commitment to yield to the other is part of the commitment to unite with the other person in building a loving, healthy, mutually fulfilling relationship.

The implicit, unavoidable commitment to surrender one's independence of will, must be recognised as the other side of the commitment to have and to hold, to love and to cherish each other. Each spouse makes a commitment to look after the rights of the other partner.

The marriage commitment is like the Christian commitment. In both relationships, we must forgo independent self-assertion for the purpose of growth together.

In the marriage-home that you are building, you want to furnish it, to decorate it, with the beauty of a loving union. Married couples can spend a lot of money on furniture and even expensive works of art; the most decorative and beautiful furnishing of their home can be their love and unity.

Jesus said that, in marriage, the two become one. It is the work of a lifetime to keep your vows, to become more and more one, out of two. We have seen how it takes an unconditional commitment, a giving of self to the other, so that each spouse gains an enlarged self as the 'we'.

Oneness comes from serving to fulfil the other, and to surrender independence of wills. Each day of your marriage you can cooperate with God to fulfil the calling of marriage:

> 'It is a lifelong union in which a man and a woman are called so to give themselves in body, mind, and spirit, and so to respond, that from their union will grow a deepening knowledge and love of each other.' (Marriage AAPB Second Form, 560)

As you build your marriage, you will need to protect it from decay and damage. How will you work to keep it in good repair?

Reflection/Discussion: The two become one—by mutual submission of wills

1. How do you each feel about surrendering your individual right to act as an independent person? Are there some areas in which you want to act independently of the other? Make a commitment to be accommodating to one another.
2. If there is an irremovable conflict of wills between you on a crucial issue, how will you resolve it?

PART 5

MAINTENANCE—KEEPING YOUR MARRIAGE IN GOOD REPAIR

Your marriage is like a house that needs regular maintenance and, sometimes, major repairs. The Christian faith has powerful help for reconciliation and renewal of relationships.

24 RESOLVING CONFLICT IN YOUR MARRIAGE

A successful marriage will not be without conflicts, but conflicts must be handled well to have a successful marriage.

Mutual companionship does not mean that there won't be disagreements, or even conflicts. Conflicts between people are a fact of life, and marriages are no exception. We must accept that conflict can be a part of married life.

Improving your skills in resolving your conflicts is a wise step before you marry. If you have enough time together before sealing the union, you will probably have some opportunities to have disagreements. This is useful training in the reality of a relationship. Use your engagement's conflicts well and learn from your disagreements.

The marriage service reminds us that one of the purposes for which God ordained matrimony is 'for the mutual companionship, help and comfort that the one ought to have of the other, both in prosperity and adversity' (Marriage AAPB First Form, 548). To become 'one' in a growing companionship of love, the couple will need to work on how they resolve their differences and disagreements.

Learn about each other before you marry

Couples get upset by arguments in the engagement period but they can be helpful, revealing problems in communication and bringing issues to the surface. This is part of learning about the real person you are going to marry.

I have been surprised on several occasions to learn from couples heading for marriage that they have not talked about various important issues about marriage. Do they both want children? How many would they want? There are many topics that should be raised.

There is great value in working through some checklists of key issues before you marry. I have used the *Prepare-Enrich* pre-marriage assessment tool with couples, which involves them separately answering questions pertinent to married life and then discussing their differences and answers. (See https://www.prepare-enrich.com.)

Learn to handle conflict constructively

How to handle and resolve marital conflicts is a vital skill to learn. In our formative years, we develop or learn our preferred ways of handling conflict, and then we bring these conflict strategies to marriage. The couple will need to work out a constructive way to resolve their important differences.

Christians should be committed to handling their conflicts well. We are called to peace, and to be peacemakers. The Bible offers much wisdom on how to be a peacemaker in relationships. Here are some principles.

1. Ask yourself: Is this worth fighting over?

Sometimes you will overlook an offence (Proverbs 19:11). We will need to let some things go and decide that the matter is not important in the big scheme of things. People are different and we should accept this fact.

My wife and I have developed a measurement scale that we each use when we have a clash of wills over an issue. We each ask ourselves: on a scale of 1 to 10 (1 being a low priority matter, 10 a critically important issue), how much do I care about this, and getting my own way? This usually solves the matter. If the issue is more important to the beloved than to self, and no big issue is involved, we let it go.

2. Get the log out of your own eye

Before you take up the faults of your partner, you might like to find out your own contributions to the problem. We all have blind-spots, which should cause us to pause and check-up within (Matthew 7:3-5).

3. Listen well and talk gently

Good communication increases the chances of clarifying differences and connecting with the feelings of each other. When you need to raise your own concerns, try to do it without blaming and simply describe how you feel and think about the matter.

4. Get help if necessary

Some problems may not be able to be sorted out between the two of you. Since you value your relationship, you can decide to get someone to help you communicate and resolve your differences. A professional counsellor or mediator will be worth the expense if this saves your marriage.

A good practical guide to resolving personal conflicts on Christian principles is found in Ken Sande, *The Peacemaker* (2004).

Prepare to deal with your conflicts

When your relationship is going well and there are few or no conflicts, it may be hard to imagine this happening. It is a good time to do some preventive work on how you deal with conflicts when they arise.

Here are a few suggestions for early prevention of problems.

Face your conflicts, don't avoid them. The Christian faith calls us to peace. However, this does not mean avoiding issues; this is a mistake often made by followers of Christ. We think that love and peace require us to give way or let matters go for the sake of peace. This is not good resolution of conflicts. We are faced with the more challenging calling to navigate our relationship through the channel bounded by Truth and Love (Ephesians 4:15).

Make an agreement with each other to deal with conflicts constructively. You can draw up a procedure to follow when you find yourselves in a serious conflict or disagreement. (The *Prepare/Enrich* assessment tool has some helpful resources in this area.)

Understand each other's 'conflict style'. Before the wedding service, gain an understanding of how you each handle conflict—your default 'conflict style'. A counsellor may be of assistance.

Create principles. Decide on a method for resolving significant differences that may arise.

Start early. Make sure you deal with important areas of conflict that may exist during your engagement.

Your 'Constructive Conflict' vow

It is a wise idea to make a commitment to one another in advance, to deal with conflicts that may come.

When you make your vows to each other, I recommend

that you consider making your own private commitment to each other that you will resolve to work to rebuild and renew your relationship if your marriage hits choppy waves.

Years ago, I received a phone call from a young American couple who were in my city on their overseas honeymoon trip. They asked to come and see me because they were having some conflict in their new marriage. The pastor who prepared them for marriage had urged them to go to a Christian counsellor or pastor for help if their marriage got into trouble.

They did exactly what he had suggested. They looked up a church and minister in the phone book, and my church and number were near the top of the list (Anglican churches under 'A', a parish starting with 'C').

We spent a few hours together as I listened to them and offered some help. They seemed encouraged and happy when they left, and I trust they have gone on well in their marriage. They were faithful followers of Christ, and they acted on the wise advice of their marriage celebrant and pastor.

Make that same commitment to each other as you get married.

Reflection/Discussion: Resolving conflict in your marriage

1. How do you handle differences and conflicts in your relationship? What are your individual conflict styles?
2. Discuss together how you can make your own private marital commitment to resolve conflicts in a constructive way.
3. Decide on a conflict resolution procedure together. Look for help from counsellors or pastoral guides who are competent in conflict resolution and communication skills.

25 FORGIVENESS AND YOUR MARRIAGE

Forgiveness is central to the Christian life and the Christian's marriage, but it may still be the hardest thing to do.

Your wedding vows may be the emotional high point of the service, but the day may come when the most important words that you say in the service may prove to be: 'Forgive us our sins, as we forgive those who sin against us.'

In little things, and sadly sometimes in the biggest betrayals of life, marriage is a test of how we can forgive each other.

Being married brings with it the possibility of being hurt by the other, sometimes deeply. *Will* you forgive? *How* can you forgive them when the hurt is deep and serious? *Should* you even forgive your spouse for some failures?

In the Christian marriage service, the couple and the congregation pray the Lord's Prayer: *Forgive us our sins as we forgive those who sin against us.* This part of the service can easily be passed over as a familiar part of Christian worship language and rattled off in rote form. The vows are dramatic and filled with emotion; the Lord's Prayer is part of the background. Yet learning to do what Jesus says in the prayer—to seek forgiveness for ourselves as we forgive those who have sinned against us—may be the key to keeping the vows.

Forgiving the other may be the hardest marriage task

By saying your vows in a Christian context, you make a commitment before God to forgive the sins of those who sin against you. You are essentially making a promise to be forgiving towards each other. This is a solemn commitment.

Forgiveness is central to the way of following Jesus Christ, and it cannot be set aside when Christians marry. Forgiving others is for the times when they hurt us and disappoint us, and marriage will provide occasions for practising the way of forgiving.

Forgiving those who hurt us is hardest when the offender is important to us, close to us. Marriage can be a place where the calling to follow Jesus Christ is most severely tested, where we must forgive the very person whose sin has hurt us so much.

The Christian way of forgiveness

For the Christian getting married, forgiveness is not an optional or minor obligation. Forgiveness is central to the Christian life and the Christian's marriage.

The practice of forgiving each other in your marriage relationship will be illuminated by your understanding of how the Christian good news of God's love in Jesus shows us the way of forgiveness. God offers us forgiveness of our sins through the life and death of Jesus Christ.

Understanding *how* forgiveness works is vital. It is not enough to believe you should forgive others; you need to know how to do it.

When it comes to the sensitive and critical challenge of

forgiveness, the Christian faith presents us with great wisdom. Here are a few insights about forgiveness from the way of Christ.

1. Forgiving others is costly and hard

Forgiveness is not just forgetting or denying the problem. It is not waiting for the other person to change or time to heal the wounds. It is not a quick fix; it is not 'kiss and make-up'. Forgiveness is not simply saying words. It is a very costly choice to follow the way of Christ in the face of your own pain.

Listen to Walter Wangerin's description of forgiving:

> 'You do deny yourself and die a little, in order to forgive. Pride dies. Fairness dies. Rights die, as do self-pity and the sweetness of a pout, or the satisfaction of a little righteous wrath. You take leave of the centre of the marriage and of your own existence. You die a little, that the marriage might rise alive.' (Wangerin, 96)

2. You will need to be very convinced about the essential importance of forgiveness

Christians have a strong reason to believe in forgiving others: we have been forgiven and we have been commanded by God to forgive others. The conviction that you have been offered forgiveness from God for your own failures, and that you need God's ongoing grace, will fuel your pursuit of a forgiving heart towards others.

3. You will need help from God to forgive

We need to find the inner strength to forgive others. Our

own self-needs and selfishness are so aroused by rejection and injustice, we can easily be dragged deeply into the vortex of our own human, natural feelings of resentment.

If the day comes when you need to forgive your spouse, you will have to draw on that other primary relationship: between you and God. You will have to go to your Head and Lord, Jesus Christ, to find the source and the power of forgiveness.

No marriage is perfect, because the spouses are not perfect. So, forgiveness will be necessary in all marriages, to varying degrees.

> 'A successful marriage is one in which two broken and forgiving people stay committed to one another in a sacrificial relationship in the face of life's chaos. True intimacy comes about only when a husband and wife are willing to be broken and to bless one another with forgiveness ... As time goes on in a marriage that operates on the principle of brokenness and forgiveness, the marriage will get stronger and stronger.' (Allender & Longman, 347)

Christian marrying couples need to embrace the way of forgiveness and learn its paths. Wise commentators on the Christian way of forgiveness have often noted that forgiveness is a process and takes time.

4. Forgiving the other who sins against us may not mean we can be reconciled with the offender

We can exercise the duty of forgiveness, releasing the other person from their moral debt towards us, but unless the problem is dealt with, and the offender shows genuine repentance, the relationship may not be reconciled.

I believe that objections to forgiving others, and difficulty in forgiving, often arise from a misunderstanding of the nature of forgiveness and how it should work in practice.

Forgiveness and reconciliation

People often get confused about forgiveness and its relationship to reconciliation.

We offer forgiveness to the offender, as an undeserved gift from us. But what if it is not received properly?

> 'Forgiveness, like any other gift, may be refused: the will to forgive must meet the will to be forgiven ... Forgiveness is not an act but an attitude: and it is ineffectual until met by a responsive attitude on the other side.' (White, 60)

This aspect of the forgiveness process is mentioned by Jesus Christ:

> 'If your brother or sister sins, warn them to stop. If they change their hearts and lives [repent], forgive them.' (Luke 17:3, CEB)

I believe that the word 'forgive' here is used by Jesus to mean 'be reconciled', as it is in our own usage. We can use the word 'forgive' to mean our releasing of someone from our own anger and resentment, as well as to refer to the restoration of relationship.

The process of forgiving someone does not close the circle of reconciliation until the offender receives the offered forgiveness properly.

The 'Forgiveness Loop'

Another way of expressing this nuance would be to say that until the offender has had a genuine change of heart and life, the process of forgiving them has not been finished. I call it 'the forgiveness loop'—the process where forgiveness offered brings a proper response of confession and change.

Forgiveness can be offered by the hurt one, a change of heart towards the offender. For reconciliation to happen, there must be a change of heart and actions (repentance) by the offender too.

Let me propose some terms for the 'forgiveness loop'. Forgiveness as a process requires '*forgivingness*' (the willingness to offer forgiveness), and '*forgivenability*' (the proper response to the offered forgiveness).

Christians should understand this process already, since it is part of the Lord's Prayer, where we pray for God to forgive us as we forgive those who sin against us (Matthew 6:12-14). This is about our daily relationship with God; we ask for forgiveness, and we must show forgiveness ourselves.

Forgiving that leads to relational restoration, therefore, has two steps: it is offered, and it must be received properly.

This situation applies particularly to the case of abuse or other serious failure in marriage. The Christian call to forgive does not mean putting up with abuse or returning to be abused again. Christians who have been abused in their marriage should not think that offering forgiveness requires them to stay vulnerable to continued abuse.

Forgiveness for reconciliation requires 'forgivenability', which is demonstrated in real change.

Reflection/Discussion: Forgiveness and your marriage

1. What do you think of the idea that forgiveness is a willing relinquishment of certain rights? Do you agree with the costly task of forgiveness, as the notes describe it?
2. Can you forgive another person but still not be reconciled with them in some circumstances?

26 WHAT BREAKS A MARRIAGE?

It may be unpleasant to think about the breakup of your marriage, but thinking about the possibility in advance is still important.

To mention the possibility of divorce at a wedding service seems inappropriate and bad form. An engaged young woman once told me not to mention the topic in my wedding sermon! This negative prospect seems out of place in such a happy, hope-filled celebration.

Like it or not, however, the Anglican marriage service does contain a serious warning about breaking up the marriage. It faces up to the realistic possibility that the marriage may not last.

You can't say that Christians are not facing up to the problems of marriage!

Echoing the words of Jesus in Matthew 19:6, the marriage service affirms that 'those whom God has joined together let not man put asunder' (Marriage AAPB Second Form, 564). This is the only reference in the Anglican marriage service to the possibility of divorce—the breaking apart of the two that have been joined into one and the ending of the marriage, while the spouses are still living.

While it is not the focus of a wedding, and an engaged couple will not want to dwell on this scenario, they should go into marriage with an understanding of how to respond in a godly way to the possibility of marriage breakdown.

Christian couples who believe that God does not want marriages to be broken should be aware of how their commitment to God relates to the issue of marriage failure.

One or both of the marrying parties may have already been through the end of a marriage by divorce, so the issue and experience of divorce is already in the background of the new marriage.

Our society in the West has become accustomed to divorce, sadly, so that many will not hesitate to find justification for getting divorced. Christians who take the Bible, their faith, and their Church seriously will find it troubling.

Let's look at this difficult matter of divorce.

Divorce: a contentious issue for the Christian churches

We must admit that the issue of divorce has been a complicated one for Christian churches. The branches of the Christian Church have had different understandings about divorce and the application of the words of Jesus.

- Some churches have held that Jesus taught the indissolubility of marriage.
- Some churches have held that there are limited permitted grounds for divorce (e.g. adultery, desertion).
- Some churches have concluded that marriages fail, but remarriage can only happen with justification on certain grounds.

- Some churches allow divorce and remarriage, whatever happened in the previous union.

It is not possible to deal with the complexities of this topic in this book, so I will present my position, which I believe is consistent with current Anglican practice and has reasoned support in the interpretation of the Bible.

I recognise that my position is not held by all theologians and churches; see H. Wayne House (ed.) *Divorce and Remarriage: Four Christian Views*, (IVP 1990).

Here is my way of understanding the reality of divorce, and how to respond to it, from a Christian perspective. (For a more detailed treatment, see Instone-Brewer, 2002 and 2003.)

1. God *intends* marriage to be a lifelong covenant union, but it is not indissoluble. Marriages can fail and come to an end

This is recognised in the Bible (Deuteronomy 24:1-4; 1 Corinthians 7:15). I believe that Jesus did not rescind the Old Testament permission for divorce or propound a new law on divorce and remarriage. Rather, He challenged a legalistic approach to divorce in His setting (Matthew 19:1-9).

Churches have been tangled up by a legalistic approach to this issue, where preoccupation with grounds for divorce turned the emphasis away from preserving the marriage, to justifying the ending of it.

2. There are sinful divorces, where violation of vows and unfaithfulness leads one partner out of the union and destroys it

Jesus exposed the hypocrisy of using the divorce law to cover what is, in effect, adultery. This is the sinful ending of the marriage (Matthew 19:9).

Many years ago, I was approached for an interview by a

woman who asked me for my opinion about her divorce situation. She was a stranger to me, so I could only respond to her account. She had been finding her marriage unsatisfying and happened to meet another man with whom she fell in love. She decided to leave her husband, and the couple divorced in due course.

Then, before she married the new man, she became a Christian and had concerns about what she had done to her marriage. She was visiting pastors to ask them for their assessment of her situation in the light of the Christian faith.

With some trepidation, I told her that I thought she had ended her marriage in the sinful way that Jesus had criticised; that she should put her new relationship on hold, and seek forgiveness from her former husband to see if they could rebuild their marriage. If this reconciliation was not possible, then a new situation would apply.

She told me that I was the only pastor who had told her what her own conscience was telling her. Others had advised her to simply move on with the new relationship. I prayed with her, and never met her again.

3. It is the hardness of human hearts that breaks the marriage bond, says Jesus (Matthew 19:8); in other words—sin

'Sin' here can cover a big range of human failures. Human fallibility, not necessarily outright sinful disobedience, is usually the problem.

There are also foolish and unnecessary divorces, where the conflicts or dissatisfaction were not handled constructively.

4. As a Christian spouse, if you find yourself in a breakdown of your marriage relationship, you are called to pursue reconciliation as far as you can (1 Corinthians 7:10-11)

Unfaithfulness to the marriage vows does not necessarily

mean the ending of the marriage; there can be forgiveness and healing of the union. I have seen, in some cases, the miracle of reconciliation after adultery and desertion, with the rebuilding of a loving union.

If the ending of the marriage was sinfully brought about or engineered in the ways that Jesus condemned in Matthew 19:7-9, there should be repentance by the offender —evidence that the sinful failures behind the break-up have been acknowledged—and some attempt at reconciliation (Retief, 153).

5. Divorce is sometimes a sad inevitability

There are situations that render married life intolerable, effectively destroying the marriage; abuse and cruelty are examples.

In this scenario, the person who ends the marriage is the abuser or cruel partner, although the formal end may be initiated by the abused spouse.

If your spouse deserts you and will not return, then, after efforts to reconcile have failed, the marriage is dead. (The apostle Paul describes this kind of situation in 1 Corinthians 7:15.)

6. Whatever the sinful circumstances which bring about divorce, the marriage is ended and the parties can remarry (1 Corinthians 7:27-28)

The statements of Jesus about divorce in the Gospels have been read to suggest no or little possibility of legitimate remarriage, but this is not the only way to construe His words in context.

He is not necessarily making a universal statement about divorce but is answering a specific question about interpreting the key passage, Deuteronomy 24:1-4. (I refer readers to Instone-Brewer, Retief, and Powers for detailed explanations.)

I hold three assumptions in my interpretation of the biblical texts:

1. The Jews, who had different views about the grounds for divorce, still believed that people could validly remarry after divorce. The divorce certificates included a statement about the right to marry again. 'Everyone in the 1st century, so far as we know, agreed that a divorcee had the right to remarry' (Instone-Brewer, 2003, 98).
2. In context, Jesus was speaking in Matthew 5 and 19 to a situation in which a man divorced his wife in order to marry another woman to whom he was attracted. In this situation, the divorce, He charged, was simply a legal cover for adultery. Jesus opposed easy, 'any-cause', unjustified divorces.
3. The apostle Paul gives advice on situations of marriage and divorce in 1 Corinthians 7, addressing his cultural and historical context: external pressures on the Church; mixed marriages between believers and disciples that led some to think they should divorce their unbelieving spouses; anti-sex/marriage views by some members. He speaks to the not-yet marrieds, the unmarried (i.e. those outside of marriage, most likely by divorce), and the widows. He is clear in his advice to the unmarried: 'If you are divorced, don't try to find a spouse. But if you do marry, you haven't sinned' (1 Corinthians 7:27-28). (See Powers, Chapter 14, for a detailed explanation.)

Summary

A Christian approach, then:

- holds a high view of marriage
- disapproves of sinful reasons for ending a marriage
- seeks reconciliation as far as it is possible
- takes responsibility for one's fault in the failure
- understands that when a marriage is ended, it must be accepted as no longer binding.

Marriages can be destroyed in bad, sad, or 'mad' (foolish) ways, but they are still ended.

Separation may occur, but before it becomes final, do all you can to be reconciled. Do not easily or quickly abandon the marriage. If time and effort prove unsuccessful in reconciling the differences that led to the separation, ask the Lord to help you find His healing for the pain. Take responsibility for your part in the problem and seek God's forgiveness—and from your former spouse, too.

The Christian spouse will do his or her best to preserve and strengthen the marriage. The best antidote to the failure of divorce is to work together to make the union strong and satisfying for each other.

The complete breakdown of a marriage does not usually come without warning signs. How can a couple prevent the breakdown of their union? How can you keep your marriage-house in good repair?

Reflection/Discussion: What breaks a marriage?

1. Make a commitment to each other about how you will respond to a serious breakdown in your relationship. Decide now that you will make every

effort to seek reconciliation and that you will each act with integrity.
2. Pray for the protection of your marriage against temptations, hardness of heart, and sinful failures.

Further reading: David Instone-Brewer, *Divorce and Remarriage in the Bible*, and *Divorce and Remarriage in the Church*; B. Ward Powers, *Marriage and Divorce: The New Testament Teaching*; Frank Retief, *Divorce*.

27 REPAIRING YOUR MARRIAGE

Your commitment in marriage includes a resolution to keep working on your relationship, to keep it in good shape.

Marriage, like a house, needs maintenance and repairs as time goes on. Couples spend a lot of money on the wedding day and honeymoon. It is always sad to see a house that has become dilapidated and fallen into disrepair, and even sadder to see a marriage deteriorate.

Why not proactively put effort into the maintenance of your marriage? Keep it in good repair before it starts to break down.

Daily recommitment

Marriage is one of those big decisions of life. You make it with a beautiful ceremony and celebration and then settle down to the routine of married life.

Let me suggest that you think of each day as the first day of your marriage, a day of commitment to love. Your marriage vows were a commitment to the constant renewal of your union. The paradox of the marriage vows is that the two become one in the wedding ceremony, consummated in sexual union, but their union is a oneness that should deepen and strengthen. They *become* one and they should continue to *grow into* oneness.

Every day of your married life is a day of recommitment to one another. You want to be a better husband; you want to be a better wife. Both of you want to be better together as a married couple. Your faithfulness to each other will be tested and challenged by life's experiences.

Your married relationship is very important to you; it defines you. You are a married couple together. While your marriage is not your whole identity, without it your identity is missing a vital part. As you work on your marriage, you are expressing your identities. Each partner has an I-We identity. I am a spouse; I am a member of a couple.

The Christian's daily recommitment to God

There is a similar I-We identity in the Christian's life. I am a Christian; I belong to Christ as His servant and friend. This is central to my identity and my living. Each day of my life, I go out based on this status of being in relationship with God through Jesus Christ. Wherever I go, I am Christ's and cannot leave this connection behind me.

The Christian knows that every day is a day of recommitment to Jesus. As a Christ-follower, this relationship with God, and in Christ, should be a growing one.

The Christian may start out at baptism making the commitment, but we know that the discipleship commitment must be daily renewed. Our obedience to Him is tested by temptation every day of our lives. Our faithfulness to God is always tested.

Your Christian life requires ongoing renewal, in prayer, fellowship, and worship.

Maintaining your marriage

Marriage is an ongoing invitation to renew our love and commitment. Let us be intentional about the reinvigoration of our vows.

Here are six methods you can use to grow closer to one another. Once again, we see how the marriage relationship and the Christian life have similar processes for maintenance and growth.

1. Keep working on your oneness

Constantly invest in your relationship as you go on together. Spend time together, despite the busyness of life and work. It is too easy to get into a rut and forget to focus on each other.

There is a parallel in the Christian life here. As the apostle Paul urges us, we must have a goal of moving forward in our faith and discipleship. If we are not pursuing the 'prize of God's upward call in Christ Jesus' (Philippians 3:13, CEB), we will begin to drift downwards and backwards. The Christian life, and the married life, both call for effort towards growth and improvement.

2. Check how you are going and growing

You can take a 'marriage health' check-up using the *Enrich* marriage assessment, a tool that gives you an insight into your relationship in key areas. A counsellor helps you complete the inventory and then provides you with feedback.

3. Develop some 'Rules of Married Life' to keep your union on track

Some Christians have adopted the discipline of a 'Rule of

Life', which is a set of habits or disciplines to follow that will give shape and strength to one's spiritual life. This may involve having time for personal prayers, reading the Bible, involvement in a church community, or some form of service to others (see Calhoun, 35).

Married couples, in a similar way, can draw up their own 'Rule of Married Life': a set of resolutions and habits to help them stay growing and close. This may involve planning regular 'dates'; special holidays; reading a book on marriage or relationships together. An uncle and aunt of mine gave us a book of reflections on marriage as a wedding gift, which we read and discussed together in the early months of our union.

The married couple know that every day they will be either moving towards each other in love or letting the relationship slide. Every day can bring a test of commitment to my spouse. You will fall into habits as a couple—why not decide on some good habits that will keep your marriage fit?

4. Consider planned time for drawing closer to one another

Life can get busy, and time together for developing your relationship can be squeezed out or forgotten among other priorities. Decide to make time to be together.

Many couples have found that attending a 'marriage enrichment/encounter' weekend is a deeply renewing activity for their relationship. There are a number of organisations that offer weekends for married couples to go away to focus on their relationship and receive encouragement. (An example: *Better Marriages*, bettermarriages.org.au.) You get plenty of time privately as a couple to communicate and there are talks and fellowship with other couples who are also drawing closer to one another.

5. Be prepared to adjust to the changes in your lives and your marriage relationship

Working on your relationship will be necessary as you move through the different seasons of your marriage, and perhaps family life. The different stages of marriage will bring new challenges and opportunities. As individuals and as a couple, life does not stay the same.

6. You can renew your vows and refresh your commitment

There is value in reviewing your wedding vows, and deciding to renew them to each other, even in front of friends. If your marriage has come through difficulties and you have rebuilt it together, you may want to start again and make those vows a second time, with a deeper insight and a mature commitment.

There is value in a public, intentional renewal of your wedding vows. From time to time, I have had the delightful task of leading married couples in a service of renewal or reaffirmation of their wedding vows.

Sometimes they do it after years of happy married life, and sometimes couples come back to a renewal after failures and the recovery of their marriage. Family and friends can then rejoice with you at the faithfulness to your vows already demonstrated. Such occasions are very joyful.

Marriage is a journey into oneness, and you need to keep moving onwards.

What can you do if your marriage collapses completely? How can you rebuild your marriage, if you both want to do so?

Reflection/Discussion: Repairing your marriage

1. The Christian should remember his/her commitment to Jesus every day. How often do you think about your marriage vows? What can you do to remind yourself about your calling to love each other?
2. Think of some ways you can draw aside to renew your marriage relationship. Perhaps: reading a book on marriage together; doing a course on marriage at a church; participating in a Marriage Enrichment weekend.

PART 6
REBUILDING YOUR MARRIAGE

Marriages fail for many reasons, but some can be put back together again on better foundations and with a new prospect of success.

28 RESTARTING YOUR MARRIAGE

When a marriage seems finished, can it be restarted?

Sometimes marriages have a crisis that runs 'the marriage carriage' off the road into a ditch. How do you rebuild a broken marriage?

'For better, for worse.' The marriage vows envisage the possibility of 'better' and 'worse' for the marrying couple. A 'worse' scenario may be a shattering difficulty that nearly destroys your marriage. It may erupt suddenly, or it may be the culmination of a long stagnation.

I believe that couples who want to be true followers of Christ will try their best to seek reconciliation and to save their marriage. Please note that I am not saying that one partner should stay and endure abuse or cruelty, if that is the problem. Many marriage collapses come about for other reasons—causes that may be corrected.

The important thing is how much both parties want to try rebuilding. This is why I suggest that separation, in many cases, should be done with a view to reconciling and reuniting.

When it looks like the marriage is over, with little hope of restoration, there are still some steps to take.

Four steps to rebuilding a marriage

1. Try to understand how the problems in your relationship developed

Some problems arise from within the personality depths of one or both partners, who are unaware of deep-seated issues that only surface as they get older. Couples who marry as young adults may be unaware of these personal issues that bubble up to roil the surface of their marriage. Then the couple must deal with these issues together.

Problems and conflicts are painful, but they also offer possibilities for deeper change and renewal. Your marriage is still alive, though wounded and in need of healing.

The crisis in your relationship may be like a red light on your car's instrument panel; something is wrong and must be fixed. Here is where your commitment to each other, to persevere and work on the problems together, becomes crucially important.

You started with high hopes, but deeper issues were not raised or recognised. Then came a 'clash' of expectations that hurt one or both. There was a desire to get past this 'pinch'; a quick fix brought the relationship back to stability. But the problem was still present, waiting to re-emerge. Finally, the repeated, unresolved issue became a 'crunch', or crisis, in the relationship. Not resolved, it can become a 'crash'.

When you try to live with an unresolved clash or crunch, stagnation sets in; the relationship begins to die, and it will cease. It can be a silent termination by one of the parties, who walks away, or a mutual agreement that it is over.

2. Beware of a premature re-commitment, which leaves the underlying problems unresolved

Some couples try again, and honestly seek to reboot their relationship.

One couple I knew had separated. Then they came to see me, and excitedly told me that they were getting back together again. I asked them a few questions about how this had happened, and it became clear to me that they had not addressed the problems. They were making a premature recommitment. I begged them not to do this, but to do more work on the problems. Sadly, they didn't do this, and they cycled back to a collapse of the marriage.

3. If the collapse of the marriage has not been caused by irreparable failure, you may consider whether it is possible to make a fresh re-boot

I believe that separation, usually the first stage in the ending of a marriage, should be done with a view to resolving problems and coming back together. Christians should be people who seek reconciliation, as far as possible, short of exposing themselves to further abuse.

Rather than walking away, a better approach is to jointly renegotiate the relationship. Go back and deal with the root problem together.

4. Re-building your marriage relationship may require the help of a marriage or relationship counsellor

Deep-seated personal problems and hard relational dysfunction may be beyond your resources to address. You may need someone to help you, someone who can come alongside both of you as a counsellor and helper.

A competent counsellor who also understands your Christian faith may be a good choice.

This would be a worthwhile investment of time and money. Your marriage is worth saving; put some money into the counselling if necessary.

For further reading, Neil T. Anderson and Charles Mylander have provided a powerful and helpful way of renewing your marriage in Christ in their book *Setting Your Marriage Free* (2014).

The Christian's life also can experience periods of stagnation, crunches of expectations, failures of discipleship, and weak foundations in the disciple's faith-understanding, as well as falls into temptation and serious backsliding. Some then give up the profession of Christian faith, abandon their baptism vows and walk away from the Lord. It looks like it is over for their relationship with God. However, sometimes the prodigal disciple comes to his/her senses and begins the journey back to the heavenly Father. The relationship with God is restored, rebooted, and hopefully on better foundations.

In the Christian life, and in the life of a marriage, there can be a fresh restart after failure.

The good news is that many couples do succeed in rebuilding their marriages. They have the satisfaction of looking back years later at how they found love and satisfaction again after a rocky patch.

When we *go through* difficulties, it is an invitation to *grow through* difficulties.

Reflection/Discussion: Restarting your marriage

1. This chapter is for people whose marriage has been through a crisis, and who are committed to

rebuilding it. Do you both understand and agree about the causes of the problem?
2. If you are having serious difficulties in your relationship, find a counsellor or pastor to help you renew the foundations of your marriage.

PART 7

HOSPITALITY—YOUR MARRIAGE AND ITS GUESTS

Your marriage is not a world of your own, although it must be your special relationship. Your marriage will have an influence on others. Your marriage-house will have its guests.

29 YOUR MARRIAGE AS A MINISTRY TO OTHERS

Your Christian marriage relationship and your home life are called to be a blessing to others.

Your home will entertain guests, and so will your marriage. Your marriage can bless others with its hospitality and witness, and you will be blessed by the presence of guests who strengthen your lives.

The focus of the marrying couple is naturally on each other, on building a world of their own. The Christian calling to married couples, however, has a bigger vision: they are serving the Lord and His world through their marriage.

Four ways a Christian marriage serves the Lord and His world

1. Good marriages are a great blessing to society, and a Christian marriage can be a strong witness to the source of Love itself, the Creator

The marriage services recognise that the married couple has a calling to serve the world through their union:

> 'Eternal God ... Make their life together a sign of Christ's love in this broken world, that unity may overcome estrangement, forgiveness heals guilt, and joy conquers despair, through Jesus Christ our Lord. Amen.' (Marriage APBA Second Order, 665)

> 'Almighty Father, giver of life and love ... strengthen their wills to keep the promises they have made; that they may live to your glory and to the good of mankind; through Jesus Christ our Lord. Amen.' (Marriage AAPB Second Form, 566)

We return to the original biblical passage about marriage, which places marriage in this very context of serving God and His world:

> 'God created humanity in God's own image, in the divine image God created them, male and female God created them.' (Genesis 1:27, CEB)

The man and the woman work together in God's world, as partners in the work God has given them both to do.

Dietrich Bonhoeffer, the famous German theologian who died at the hands of the Nazis, wrote a wedding sermon for friends, from his prison cell. He stated the ministry calling of the married couple in these words:

> 'Marriage is more than your love for each other. It has a higher dignity and power, for it is God's holy ordinance, through which He wills to perpetuate the human race till the end of time. In your love you see only your two selves in the world, but in marriage you are a link in the chain of the generations, which God causes to come and to pass away to His glory, and calls into His kingdom. In your love you see only the heaven of your own happiness, but in marriage you are placed at a post of responsibility towards the world and mankind. Your love is your own private possession, but marriage is more than something personal—it is a status, an office.' (Bonhoeffer, 41)

Your marriage serves the good of humankind and the kingdom of God in several ways.

2. Family life is a key area of service to the world

Your children are the VIP guests of your marriage.

Their lives depend on your relationship and the 'home' (family) you have built for yourselves and for them. Your marriage is not for yourselves alone. It is a service to your children.

God designed marriage for the creation and nurture of persons (Psalm 127). The task of marriage is to create a healthy relationship that provides a healthy environment for the creation and nurture of children. Is there a more strategic and vital task than the raising of our children in love and wisdom?

As parents you have a responsibility to provide care and examples for your children. The father is the first model of a man for his sons and his daughters. The mother models womanhood for her daughters and sons, in the home and outside it.

The special bond of marriage does not easily accommodate a third party into it. Those outside the marriage are warned explicitly not to get between the two, not to separate them (Matthew 19:6). Children, however, who are the fruit of the union of the two, are a third party whose presence expresses and hopefully bonds the two parents closer together, enfleshing in a wonderful way their love for each other. In their children, the love of the couple creates new love and being.

Parents look at their children, the fruit of their love-union, and see in this new little person, part of each other in a new, blended embodiment.

Strive to stay in love and care towards each other so that the children will see and experience the blessing of a loving home.

3. Your marriage provides the spiritual environment for your family, modelling what it means to be Christian, and to serve God

Christians know that we are called to be examples and models for others, showing them what Christ is like and how we are to shine as lights in the world. This begins at home and in our marriages. Parents model for their children what faith in God means in everyday life. Let us not fail here.

Marriage counsellors know that each person usually brings to their marriage the memory of a marriage that they watched from the front row seats, as children. These are 'ghost' marriages that haunt the new union. We have a ringside seat at a marriage long before we get married ourselves.

What will our children learn from their experience of watching our marriage?

Your marriage relationship will be a model, for example, to

your children of what marriage, and specifically, a Christian marriage, is like. Will it be a good example?

Christian parents have a responsibility to help their children understand the things of God. Our witness of love for each other will give power to our words and exhortations. No parent is perfect, but if the gap between what we profess and how we act is too great, the children will see the hypocrisy.

4. Christians who are married are also involved in the great commission of Jesus Christ—to make disciples (Matthew 28:18-20)

Your marriage and the family life that is associated with it will be part of your calling to serve God and the world. Married couples are called to minister the gospel to people who meet them (Acts 18:24-26). Some of the best evangelism is done through loving, godly marriages; the early church met in homes.

In the Anglican marriage services, from Matrimony BCP (1662) onwards, several Psalms from the Bible are set for use. Psalm 67 is one of these set biblical songs. It is a prayer that God may bless His people that His ways 'may be known upon earth, (His) salvation among all nations'. It envisions the people of God as a channel of blessing to the whole world, so that all the ends of the earth will reverence God.

The inclusion of this psalm in the Anglican marriage service reminds the couple and the community of faith that they are part of God's plan to serve the world and spread abroad the good news of His salvation, to be a means for the joyous praise of God everywhere. It is a shame that this psalm is often omitted from many Anglican wedding services because the ceremony loses this world-encompassing vision of marriage as a blessing to the world.

Your marriage is about more than each of you, or even about your family.

Your marriage can be a witness and mode of service to the community and the world.

Reflection/Discussion: Your marriage as a ministry to others

1. How will you serve God and His world through your marriage?
2. Pray about the early years of your marriage as you minister as parents. Ask God to grant you a sound foundation for nurturing your children.

30 YOUR MARRIAGE AND THE POWER OF GOD

In a Christian marriage, the couple have a mutual relationship with the Lord God, who is a source of help beyond our resources or imaginations.

Every house needs power. Your marriage will have the energy of your natural love for each other. There is also an available source of supernatural power, from God by His Spirit.

A Christian marriage ceremony is surrounded by prayer to the Lord, the Maker of marriage. The marriage that starts with prayer should continue in prayer, and perhaps even survive by prayer.

Let's consider how your marriage needs the ministry of prayer.

Marriages need divine help!

The couple comes before God and other witnesses to call upon Him for His blessing on their union and His help for their life together. They make their vows in the setting of prayer, with a congregation joining them to ask God's blessing.

'God the Father enrich you with his grace, God the Son make you holy in his love, God the Holy Spirit strengthen you with his joy. The Lord bless you and keep you in eternal life.' (Marriage AAPB Second Form, 564)

This should not be treated as a formality. Every married couple knows how challenging the task of being successfully married can prove. The promises of marriage need to be fulfilled over the long haul, in good times and in times of stress and difficulty.

A woman, long widowed, told me that she had discovered prayer early in her married life when her husband's drinking problem was spoiling their lives. She turned to God in desperate prayer, the problem lifted, and decades of happy marriage followed. When she could not help her husband, she turned to God. Prayer became very real for her, not a formality left behind when the wedding ceremony finished.

The couple should be praying earnestly to God for His strength and wisdom for their life together. Here is a prayer to be said by the wedding couple themselves, at the taking of their vows:

'God of tenderness and strength, you have brought our paths together and led us to this day; go with us now as we travel through good times, through trouble, and through change. Bless our home, our partings, and our meetings. Make us worthy of one another's best, and tender with one another's dreams. Amen.' (Marriage APBA Second Order, 662)

Prayer as the best gift for the couple

Beyond all the lovely gifts given to the couple, the prayers of their community may be the most valuable gift of all. The casserole dishes will break in time; the linen and towels will wear out; but the gift of prayers for the couple may have a lifelong impact.

Prayers are offered in the wedding for the blessings of God on the marriage, such as children, faithfulness, growing companionship, and the blessing of others through this union. Psalm 67 and other songs can be sung, to express the prayer that God will bless the couple so that they can be a blessing to the world.

The Christian couple and their friends will not regard prayers in the wedding service as a fringe matter, or a formality.

Let us keep praying for the newly married couple beyond the wedding day! Ask your praying friends to intercede for your union, for protection, love, and perseverance.

Make prayer together part of your married life

The marriage that starts with prayer should grow in prayer. As the old saying goes: 'The family that prays together stays together.' Let the couple make prayer a source of inspiration and power for their relationship and their family.

Most married couples sooner or later face problems that seem beyond them, and they can become desperate. I have sat and listened to couples and families in real pain and perplexity. The couple can be at the end of their own resources. Prayer can become a lifeline for a drowning couple or parents. What was a formal or unimportant part of life suddenly becomes a powerful resource.

- Through prayer, we can get wisdom from God where our own abilities fail us (James 1:5-7).
- As you pray, God's Spirit can show you what He wants you to know and to do (Romans 8:26-27).

I think it is a shame that in recent years, couples attending church and professing faith in Christ have been marrying in services that have abbreviated some elements of prayer.

Some of the prayers in the marriage service will reflect the need for 'healing of memories' for hurts of the past, lest they block the path to future happiness and service.

What place will prayer have in your married life? It can be a main pillar of your marriage, as you seek God together for wisdom, strength, and help. Your relationship with God, strongly flourishing in your prayer life, will help your marriage.

I believe that when the children come, and particularly in their teenage years, the prayer life of their parents can become very urgent and necessary.

Watch out for the relationship issues that block your prayers

A problem in your marriage may become a problem in your prayers and in your relationship with God.

God sees our relationship to other people as connected to our relationship with Himself. The two great commandments —to love the Lord our God and to love our neighbour as ourselves—are really one command. A failure to show proper love to our closest 'neighbour'—our spouse—may be a sign of a problem in our attitude to God, and this will show up in our prayers with each other and for each other.

The apostle Peter challenges husbands with this sobering thought:

> 'Husbands, likewise, submit by living with your wife in ways that honor her, knowing that she is the weaker partner. Honor her all the more, as she is also a coheir of the gracious care of life. Do this so that your prayers won't be hindered.' (1 Peter 3:7, CEB)

New Testament scholar Wayne Grudem notes: 'So concerned is God that Christian husbands live in an understanding and loving way with their wives, that He interrupts His relationship with them when they are not doing so' (Grudem, 146). It will be hard to be united in prayer together to the Lord if you are not treating each other well. The Lord will want us to put things right as we come to pray.

Praying for one another, and with one another, can be a great help to making your marriage work well, and when your marriage is working well, it will greatly help your praying for one another and with another.

One final aspect of marriage for Christ-followers remains to be considered. The most important guest in your marriage is the Lord Himself, the Creator of marriage and our Saviour.

Reflection/Discussion: Your marriage and the power of God

1. How will you make prayer together and for each other a part of your married life? Have you discussed the place of Christian worship and fellowship in your married life?
2. Why not ask some godly friends to become prayer supporters for you as a couple? Your Christian friends might be praying for you already, but it would be good to ask some to uphold you particularly in prayer.

31 YOUR MARRIAGE AND GOD: THE THREE-PLY CORD

A Christian marriage is a relationship in which the union is strengthened and blessed by the living presence of the Lord God by His Spirit.

You may have seen this plaque on the walls of some Christian homes, which reminds readers of the presence of Christ in the home:

> 'Christ is the Head of this house; the Unseen Guest at every meal; the Silent Listener to every conversation.'
> (Source unknown)

Your marriage is a special, intimate form of companionship, and a marriage between Christians—followers of Jesus Christ as their Lord—is a distinct form of married companionship, since it is a relationship that is enveloped in a shared companionship with God.

Throughout these reflections, we have been looking at how the Christian faith and way of life throws light on the way of marriage. Let's close these studies by considering how knowing God can be part of your marriage.

The marriage service emphasises the calling of companionship in marriage—the mutual help and comfort that the partners have in each other:

> 'In the joys and sorrows of life, in prosperity and adversity, they share their companionship, faithfulness and strength.' (Marriage AAPB Second Form, 560)

The marriage service also places your married companionship into the sphere of your joint, shared relationship with God. This is expressed in the prayers for the couple:

> 'God the Father enrich you with his grace, God the Son make you holy in his love, God the Holy Spirit strengthen you with his joy. The Lord bless you and keep you in eternal life.' (Marriage AAPB Second Form, 564)

> '...that they and their children may come to know you in their lives and give you praise and honour; through Jesus Christ our Lord. Amen.' (Marriage AAPB Second Form, 566)

The marriage service warns at the beginning about the interference of third parties in the marriage. There is one third party to your marriage, however, whose presence should be welcome, if you want a Christian marriage: the Lord Jesus Christ Himself, the 'unseen guest' in your home.

In the biblical book of Ecclesiastes, the Teacher depicts the value of friendship in some famous words:

> 'Two are better than one because they have a good return for their hard work. If either should fall, one can pick up the other. But how miserable are those who fall and don't have a companion to help them up!

Also, if two lie down together, they can stay warm. But how can anyone stay warm alone? Also, one can be overpowered, but two together can put up resistance. A three-ply cord doesn't easily snap.' (Ecclesiastes 4:9-12, CEB)

Many have noted the reference to a 'three-ply cord' in this praise of friendship between two. Christians have often seen a veiled allusion to the presence of God (the third party) in a companionship between two. As they help each other, especially in a marriage, they have the added strengthening of a third companion in their relationship, drawing the couple closer together: the Lord God, the Creator of marriage and the source of Love.

Your love for the Lord and your love for one another

Research on marriage has noted how important are shared spiritual and religious values to the stability of the union. Before couples marry, they should consider the place of religious beliefs and practices in their relationship.

Let us consider, as we close these studies, the positive influence of a shared Christian faith between the couple. You are marrying 'in the Lord', as devoted followers of Jesus Christ. You may not have thought how practical a help for your marriage faith in God could be.

I am speaking of a *real* experience of the gracious love of God, not just formal church attendance or affiliation. I am talking about the real presence of the Lord in the life of the couple, and their family.

How will your Christian lives enrich your marriage?

Let me mention three main areas of help that God can bring your marriage.

1. Your spiritual bond can strengthen your marriage union

Getting married and growing together is like building a house together (metaphorically). You are constructing something—your life together. The facets of your relationship will become the building blocks of your union.

Sharing a strong, vital faith in God will be another supporting part of your relationship. The couple that prays together is more likely to stay together. If you are members of a healthy church community, this fellowship can be another support.

For the companionship of the Lord to be real for both of you, it must be important to each of you individually. It is common for one partner to be more spiritually interested than the other. If the gap widens too far, what could be a uniting factor only becomes a point of difference. Thankfully, the reverse also happens: the faith of one partner in time draws the other to God (1 Peter 3:1-2; 1 Corinthians 7:13-14).

If you or your partner are getting married in a Christian service but do not have a real or strong personal faith in Christ yourselves, I encourage you to think about how the companionship of God may enrich your companionship with one another.

Your marriage commitment is to become one with each other. If your spouse has a strong faith in God, this is a reason to better understand what faith in God means.

Another way your Christian faith can help your marriage is by allowing your relationship to be directed by the love of Christ. You are married partners; you are also fellow children of God. You have a mutual relationship of love and respect as followers of Christ.

2. Follow Jesus Christ and His ways, to avoid bad behaviour

When your marriage relationship falls into disharmony

and conflict, you are not permitted by the Lord to give way to ungodly behaviour. Your attitude and actions must always stay on the level of love (1 Corinthians 13). Sadly, Christians experiencing marriage problems can sometimes fall below the standard of love in their attitudes towards each other. We always owe our spouse the debt of love (Romans 13:8).

This obligation is in keeping with the blessing of the marriage service:

> 'God the Father lovingly enfold you, God the Son grace your home and table, God the Holy Spirit crown you with joy and peace.
>
> The Lord bless you and keep you in eternal life. Amen.' (Marriage APBA Second Order, 662)

3. You have the resourceful help of God in your life together

A Christian marriage should be surrounded by prayers, particularly by the praying of Christian friends and the church community. This is why a wedding service is set in a form of church worship.

I have heard of a couple who chose to have their wedding in the context of a normal Sunday worship service. At a point in the usual worship gathering, the couple stood up and came forward for their vows and the prayers of the community. This is certainly unusual, but it illustrates the point that a Christian wedding is an action of worship and prayer involving the community, not just the couple and their families.

There is a huge difference between a belief in God that is perfunctory and peripheral to your everyday life, and a living trust in the real presence and power of God. The couple who look to God for help and guidance, with strong faith, may see answers to prayer that make a difference in everyday life.

The importance of prayer in the life of the Christian

married couple can be seen in a sentence from Scripture (Psalm 20:2,4), set to be used at an Anglican marriage service:

> 'May the Lord send you help from the holy place, and give you support from Zion. May He grant you your heart's desire, and fulfil all your plans.' (Marriage AAPB Collects and Readings at a Marriage, 292)

What place will prayer have in your marriage? Will you worship God together, and belong to a supportive community of faith? Will you seek to grow in wisdom from God, as the marriage service prays?

> 'Bless N and N with wisdom and pleasure. Be their friend and companion in joy, their comfort in need and in sorrow.' (Marriage APBA Second Order, 658)

Sharing life together, in good times and in bad times, will bring to most couples their share of problems and perplexities. This is material for real, intense prayer asking God to help.

Two prayers for our marriage

My wife and I have seen some wonderful answers to our prayers over the years of our marriage. We have felt that the Lord was right there with us to help us in our times of need.

As I reflect on the place of prayer in our marriage together, I recall our wedding in August 1977. We chose two biblical prayers for inclusion in our service.

My bride chose a hymn for our wedding service, a prayer for God's blessing on our lives, which I believe God has been answering.

It was composed by the Reverend John Newton (based on the blessing prayer of St Paul in 2 Corinthians 13:13):

> May the grace of Christ our Saviour
>   and the Father's boundless love,
>   with the Holy Spirit's favour,
>   rest upon us from above.
>   Thus may we abide in union
>   with each other and the Lord,
>   and possess, in sweet communion,
>   joys which earth cannot afford.

We also chose, from the set wedding passages, one of the apostle Paul's great prayers in his letter to the Ephesians. This prayer is intended for Christians generally but has strong relevance to a couple getting married.

I recall listening to this inspiring prayer, alongside my bride, and to the exhortation of the minister as he explained its relevance to us.

> 'This is why I kneel before the Father. Every ethnic group in heaven or on earth is recognized by him. I ask that he will strengthen you in your inner selves from the riches of his glory through the Spirit. I ask that Christ will live in your hearts through faith. As a result of having strong roots in love, I ask that you'll have the power to grasp love's width and length, height and depth, together with all believers. I ask that you'll know the love of Christ that is beyond knowledge so that you will be filled entirely with fullness of God. Glory to God, who is able to do far beyond all that we could ask or imagine by his power at work within us; glory to him in the church and in Christ Jesus for all generations, forever and always. Amen.' (Ephesians 3:14-21, CEB)

This prayer is not a small, mundane petition. It asks for

big things, and for an electric and expansive experience of the reality of God.

The prayer asks God to strengthen the couple in their inner selves by His Spirit, so that Christ will dwell or live in their hearts through faith, and that with this Divine love indwelling them, they will be able to grasp the vast dimensions of God's love, and to be filled with knowledge of it.

The end of this prayer is that they will have an experience of God doing in them and for them more than they ask, or could even imagine, with His great power, to God's glory.

For the wedding of one of our daughters, the couple also chose this passage, and I had the honour of preaching about its meaning for them. I composed in advance this poem-version of Paul's prayer, which I used in that wedding service and gave to them as a gift:

> May God the Father bless you from above
>   With His Spirit's power to grow in grace and love.
>   May Jesus Christ become your household guest,
>   Who comes to stay and always brings the best.
>   May true faith in Christ to help and guide
>   Equip you with the power to ride
>   To higher views of God's unbounded ways,
>   And fullness of His love through all your days.
>   May the Lord whose mighty strength
>   By far exceeds the height and length
>   Of all your hopes and plans so bold,
>   Whose fullness the very universe can't hold—
>   May our great God so work in you,
>   That all who know you well, will praise Him too!
>
> R.G. BOWLES

God is able and keen to give you blessings in your

marriage that go beyond your expectations, and to God be the glory.

Reflection/Discussion: Your marriage and God: the three-ply cord

1. In these studies, we have looked at different ways that relationship with God can throw light on marriage and your relationship. Which parallels have registered with you most strongly?
2. As you start out building your married life in its routines, how can you include God in your relationship and life together? Think of some practical ways you can make space for a spiritual fellowship with God together.

FINAL THOUGHTS

Thank you for putting in the time to read and discuss this material. You have made an investment in your coming marriage.

I hope that you have found this study of marriage in the Christian Church's understanding to be helpful to you as you move towards your wedding, or in your review of your married life.

I have written this book because I believe that the health and well-being of people and society is influenced strongly by the quality of our marriages.

I believe that a good marriage that lasts is a great blessing for women and men, and the children they may produce.

In these studies, we have seen that there are many points of connection and harmony between the characteristics of a good marriage, and the Christian way of faith and life.

When you come close to a good, successful marriage, you will hear playing the beautiful themes of love, grace, forgiveness, commitment, sacrifice, personal growth, and service. These same melodies of love can be heard, in a different key, in the good news of Christ and the way of following Him.

Understand what marriage is about, and you will get a picture of what the Christian faith is about.

I also pray that the Lord blesses you in your marriage!

Ralph G. Bowles
2025

REFERENCES AND READING

Marriage services

The marriage services referred to in these studies are the following authorised services in the Anglican Church of Australia:

The Form of Solemnization of Matrimony, *The Book of Common Prayer, for the Church of England*, (1662 and many subsequent editions). Cited as Matrimony BCP.

A Service for Marriage, First Form, *An Australian Prayer Book*, (AIO, Sydney, 1978), 548. Cited as Marriage AAPB First Form.

A Service for Marriage, Second Form, *An Australian Prayer Book*, (AIO, Sydney, 1978), 560. Cited as Marriage AAPB Second Form.

A Service for Marriage, First Order, *A Prayer Book for Australia*, (Broughton Books, Sydney,1995), 646. Cited as Marriage APBA First Order.

A Service for Marriage, Second Order, *A Prayer Book for Australia*, (Broughton Books, Sydney, 1995), 655. Cited as Marriage APBA Second Order.

Other services

Morning Prayer, First Form, *An Australian Prayer Book*, (AIO, Sydney, 1978), 22. Cited as Morning Prayer AAPB First Form.

A Service for the Public Baptism of Infants to be Used in the Church, Second Order, *An Australian Prayer Book*, (AIO, Sydney, 1978), 517. Cited as Public Baptism of Infants AAPB Second Order.

A Service for the Public Baptism of Adults and Those Able to Answer for Themselves, First Order *An Australian Prayer Book*, (AIO, Sydney, 1978), 506. Cited as Adult Baptism AAPB First Order.

Other reading

Dan B. Allender & Tremper Longman, *Intimate Allies*, (Tyndale House, 1995).

Neil T. Anderson & Charles Mylander, *Setting Your Marriage Free*, (Bethany House Publishers, 2014).

Neil T. Anderson, *The Christ-Centered Marriage*, (Regal, 1996).

David Atkinson, *To Have and to Hold: The Marriage Covenant and the Discipline of Divorce*, (Collins, London, 1979).

Matthew W. Bates, *Gospel Allegiance*, (Brazos Press, Grand Rapids, Michigan, 2019).

Dietrich Bonhoeffer, 'A Wedding Sermon from a Prison Cell', *Letters and Papers from Prison*, Eberhard Bethge (ed.), (SCM Press, 1971).
Dietrich Bonhoeffer, *Life Together*, (SCM Press, 1954, 1998).
Geoffrey W. Bromiley, *God and Marriage*, (Wm. B. Eerdmans, Grand Rapids, Michigan, 1980).
Adele Ahlberg Calhoun, *Spiritual Disciplines Handbook*, (IVP, 2005).
Gary Chapman, *The Five Love Languages*, (Northfield Publishing, 1995).
Howard J. Clinebell & Charlotte H. Clinebell, *The Intimate Marriage*, (Harper-SanFrancisco, 1970).
Alan Craddock, *Being Married*, (Prepare/Enrich, 1994).
Misha Crawford and Mark Butler, 'A Match Made in Heaven: Uniting Christianity and Marital Sexuality' https://publicsquaremag.org/media-education/pop-culture/a-match-made-in-heaven-uniting-christianity-marital-sexuality
Leighton Ford, *The Attentive Life: Discerning God's Presence in All Things*, (IVP Books, Downers Grove, Illinois, 2008).
Sherif Girgis, Ryan T. Anderson, Robert P. George, *What is Marriage? Man and Woman: A Defense*, (Encounter Books, New York/London, 2012).
Thomas Gordon, *Parent Effectiveness Training*, (New American, 1975).
Jonathan Grant, *Divine Sex: A Compelling Vision for Christian Relationships in a Hypersexualized Age*, (Brazos Press, Grand Rapids, 2015).
James Greteman, *Creating A Marriage*, (Paulist Press, 1993).
Wayne Grudem, *The First Epistle of Peter: An Introduction and Commentary*, (IVP, 1988).
Douglas J. Hall, *Imaging God*, (Eerdmans, 1986).
H. Wayne House (ed.), *Divorce and Remarriage: Four Christian Views*, (IVP, 1990).
David Instone-Brewer, *Divorce and Remarriage in the Bible: The Social and Literary Context*, (Wm. B. Eerdmans, Michigan, 2002).
David Instone-Brewer, *Divorce and Remarriage in the Church*, (Paternoster, Cumbria, UK, 2003).
John Henry Jowett, *The High Calling: Meditations on St Paul's Letter to the Philippians*, (Andrew Melrose, London, 1909).
Leon R. Kass, 'Man and Woman: An Old Story', *First Things*, Institute on Religion and Public Life, Number 17, November 1991.
Robert Law, *The Tests of Life: A Study of the First Epistle of John*, (Baker Books, Michigan, 1909, 1968).
H.R. Mackintosh, *The Christian Experience of Forgiveness*, (Nisbet & Co. Ltd, London, 1954).
Mike Mason, *The Mystery of Marriage*, (Marc Europe, 1985).
Iain McGilchrist, *The Matter with Things: Our Brains, Our Delusions and the Unmaking of the World*, Volume I, The Ways to Truth, (Perspectiva Press, London, 2021).

John Newton, 'May the Grace of Christ my Saviour', https://hymnary.org/text/may_the_grace_of_christ_our_savior_newto

James Olthuis, *I Pledge You My Troth: A Christian View of Marriage, Family, Friendship*, (Harper & Row, 1976).

Ronald W. Pierce, Rebecca Merrill Groothuis, & Gordon D. Fee, *Discovering Biblical Equality: Complementarity Without Hierarchy*, (Intervarsity Press, 2005).

B. Ward Powers, *Marriage and Divorce: The New Testament Teaching*, (Family Life Movement, 1987).

Prepare-Enrich, *The Prepare/Enrich Inventory*, https://www.prepare-enrich.com.

Marriage and the Public Good: Ten Principles, The Witherspoon Institute, (Princeton, New Jersey, 2008).

Frank Retief, *Divorce: Hope for the Hurting*, (Christian Focus, Scotland, 2001).

Ken Sande, *The Peacemaker*, (Baker Books, Grand Rapids, Michigan, 2004).

Gary Smalley & John Trent, *Love is a Decision*, (Inspirational Press, 1996).

Bruce Stevens, *Regaining Intimacy: Dealing with the Pain of a Broken Relationship*, (Random House, 1995).

William K. Summers, *Building the House of Marriage*, (Robert Erdmann Publishing, CA, 1991).

Jim Talley, *Reconcilable Differences: Mending Broken Relationships*, (Tyndale, 1985).

Jim Talley & Bobbie Reed, *Too Close, Too Soon*, (Thomas Nelson, Nashville, 1982).

Very Well Mind, *The Four Stages of Relationships*, https://www.verywellmind.com/the-four-stages-of-relationships-4163472 2023.

Walter Wangerin, *As For Me and My House*, (Thomas Nelson, 1990).

Douglas White, *Forgiveness and Suffering: A Study of Christian Belief*, (Leopold Classic Library, CUP reprint, 1913).

Dallas Willard, *Hearing God: Developing a Conversational Relationship with God*, (IVP Books, Downers Grove, Illinois, 2012).

Bruce W. Winter, *Roman Wives, Roman Widows: The Appearance of New Women and the Pauline Communities*, (William B Eerdmans Publishing Co., Grand Rapids, Michigan, 2005).

THANKS

I am grateful for the privilege of being involved with many engaged couples in their journey towards their wedding, and for the discussions I have had over the years with many married partners, about their joys and struggles.

Thank you to the friends who read this book in its earlier draft and made helpful suggestions.

Thank you very much to Belinda Pollard, my editor, from Small Blue Dog Publishing. Without Belinda's guidance and valuable help, this book would not be here.

My loving and heartfelt thanks go to my wife, Sylvia, who has really written the book of marriage with me since 1977. Although she has not co-written this book or worked on the material with me, I feel as if she has been its main contributor.

Thanks be to our God, and our Lord Jesus Christ, the Designer and inspirer of marriage and the fountain of Love itself.

Ralph G. Bowles
January 2025

ABOUT THE AUTHOR

Ralph G. Bowles has served churches in Sydney, Brisbane, and the Sunshine Coast, Australia (1980-2023). He has been involved in university student work, inner city ministry, parish service in outer metropolitan and regional settings, and as a Church Health consultant for the Anglican Church Southern Queensland.

Ralph has been married to Sylvia since 1977. They have three adult children and five grandsons.

ralphbowles.com

www.ingramcontent.com/pod-product-compliance
Lightning Source LLC
Chambersburg PA
CBHW071236070526
44583CB00017B/2210